# THE ESTHER STRATEGY

# THE
# ESTHER
# STRATEGY

JANE TAYLOR

To Maybug, Kevin, Brenda, Matt, Athena, Chris,
Beth, Mark, Claire, Alan, Dan
and most importantly of all
to the glory of God
≈

Published by Zaccmedia
www.zaccmedia.com
info@zaccmedia.com

Published February 2020
Copyright © 2020 Janice Taylor

ISBN: 978-1-911211-93-8

British Library Cataloguing-in-Publication Data.
A catalogue record for this book is available from the British Library.

# CONTENTS

# INTRODUCTION

Esther is at first glance an unusual book to have been included in the Bible because God is not spoken of directly by name anywhere in its pages. This has meant that at points in history the book was not seen by Christians as having any real significance, and that is still the case in some circles even today. Yet it is a story full of spiritual truth, some of which I will unpack in the following chapters. I hope that by the time you have read this book you will understand something of its value in our journey into God's heart for us.

This is the third book that I have written over the last couple of years. With each one there have been changes in the way I write as I have grown as a writer and my style has developed. This is the first book in which I have not put all the Scripture references in the main body of the text. I originally did so because I particularly wanted to encourage readers to look up the Bible verses involved. But it has now reached the point where the verses referenced are so numerous they could be a distraction rather than a help. Having said that, I have left some key verses in the text and would encourage you to look these up – and, if possible, the other references listed at the end of each chapter.

This is also the first book in which I discuss the history of my subject. Whilst I love history, I know that not everyone does. So I have kept the background information to a minimum, but some is needed to help us to recognise and understand the truths contained within the story of Esther.

To me the Bible is a bit like an onion: the more time you spend in reading and studying it, the more you realise that there is layer upon layer of truth hidden in its pages waiting to be discovered. I have been a Christian for over thirty years now and am very conscious that whilst I obviously have a certain amount of knowledge and understanding of the Bible, there is even more that has yet to be revealed to me. Such revelation does not come through academic study, although that can prepare us for it, but by developing our relationship with God. This is because it is in moments of intimacy with Him that the truth of His Word comes alive for us and our understanding of it grows – as of course does the wisdom to apply it properly.[1]

Doing some reading about hermeneutics, which teaches the principles for understanding and applying God's Word, can be of benefit in this process, although it is not essential. The core hermeneutical principle for beginning to unlock the truths contained within the Bible is understanding the context of the book, letter or whatever that you are looking at. This is because a text out of context can become a pretext. In other words, we need to let the Word of God shape our thinking,[2] rather than looking for and using verses in it to justify what we think.[3]

Looking at the context of passages and verses in the Bible involves, for example:

- finding out who wrote the book as well as their purpose in doing so;
- looking at the historical and cultural background;

*'For I know the plans
I have for you,'
declares the LORD,
'plans to prosper you
and not to harm you,
plans to give you hope
and a future.'*

JEREMIAH 29:11

It is not wrong for us to feel a certain amount of satisfaction, or even pleasure, in our achievements, or other people's, but when we start thinking we are better than other people that is wrong, just like false humility is. An unwillingness to admit our mistakes and being unwilling to do anything to put things right are also issues of pride. Not only that; when we seek to do things our way, rather than God's, that too is a form of pride[10] because we are saying we know better than Him. Moreover, wherever there is complacency, arrogance, or rebellion of any kind, pride will be an issue too.

In the book of Revelation we are told that our enemy, the devil, was cast out of heaven after he lost the war that he had instigated.[11] He started this war because, as the prophets Isaiah and Ezekiel clearly show us, he wanted to exalt himself above God.[12] Indeed some theologians think that pride is at the root of all sin, but there are other opinions, and any Biblically based perspective is worth looking at should you want to investigate this further.

The opposite to pride is humility, as Paul says in Philippians 2:1–4:

*If you have any encouragement from being united with Christ, if any comfort from his love, if any fellowship with the Spirit, if any tenderness and compassion, then make my joy complete by being like-minded, having the same love, being one in spirit and purpose. Do nothing out of selfish ambition or vain conceit, but in humility consider others better than yourselves. Each of you should look not only to your own interests, but also to the interests of others.*

These verses make plain the need for us to have an attitude of humility, and this is something that Jesus never stopped modelling to His disciples when He was here on earth.[13] It is vital for us all to remember that, as can be seen from Philippians 2:5–11, becoming more like Jesus and doing the things that He did is the main aim of the Christian life. Just as important is remembering that we will never get there in our own strength – that we need to partner with the Holy Spirit in what will be a lifelong process of transformation.[14] In the quotation above, we are also encouraged to put others before ourselves, rather than just living a life that is focused on us and our needs.[15] This is how true humility is enacted and expressed in our lives.

One of the keys involved in this process is spending time in 'the Word', God's plumb line of truth, and asking the Holy Spirit to enable us to apply it to our lives in whatever way is appropriate for us, so that it can change us. Such a prayer will mean that the Holy Spirit can then use Scripture to:

- convict us of our sin and bring us to repentance;[16]
- counsel and guide us;[17]
- reveal the lies that we have believed and enable us to replace them with the truth;[18]
- speak to us about the future.[19]

Going back to the story of Esther, we read that King Xerxes was very angry about Vashti's disobedience to him. He discussed what had happened in depth with those closest to him – noblemen who understood the implications of her actions in terms of the legal and social framework of his empire.[20]

Whilst it is not wrong to get angry about things such as injustice, the Bible makes it plain to us that we need to be careful about how long we let our anger fester and what we do as a consequence of it.[21] This is because anger can be very destructive, particularly if we allow it to control us, and the results of it, if left unchecked, can be devastating not only to us but also to all those involved in the outworking of it. Moreover, it can completely derail the life of the person who lets their anger go unchecked, as well as the lives of those caught up in its maelstrom.

In the following incident from the life of Jesus, we can see a good example of 'righteous anger':

> *Jesus entered the temple area and drove out all who were buying and selling there. He overturned the tables of the money-changers and the benches of those selling doves. 'It is written,' he said to them, "My house will be called a house of prayer," but you are making it a "den of robbers".*

(Matthew 21:12–13)

From this we can see that righteous anger is expressed by taking whatever action is right in order to deal with a situation of injustice. Such action obviously should not involve making threats, violence, lying, or mistreating people in any way.

It seems from what we are told about Xerxes' reaction to Vashti's disobedience to him that his approach was quite measured, but only God knows for certain whether he wanted to deal with things differently. Certainly, the fact that he sought counsel from people who had the knowledge and wisdom to advise him properly shows us that he did not want to be seen as unreasonable in his response to Vashti's behaviour. Having people that we can go to for advice and counsel when we are making important decisions about our lives can be just as valuable to us[22] as it was to Xerxes, particularly if those people are more mature believers and are willing to seek the counsel of God on our behalf. In fact, such individuals are worth their weight in gold, so if you do not have people like that in your life perhaps you should think about asking God to give you some.

Let us now look at the actual question that Xerxes asked his advisers, to see what we can learn from it:

*According to law, what must be done to Queen Vashti? ... She has not obeyed the command of King Xerxes that the eunuchs have taken to her.*

(Esther 1:15)

The way in which Xerxes poses this question makes it look as if he has separated out his feelings from the legal implications of Vashti's actions. This may have been intentional, or it may have been a cultural thing, but nevertheless we can learn a lesson from it: when we need to make decisions about our lives, it is important to see them from another, perhaps more objective perspective, before looking at them subjectively. This of course is where having other people to discuss things with is beneficial. They can help us look at things differently because their perspective will obviously be far more objective than ours.

Looking again at the subject of disobedience, the Bible has a lot to say on how we should behave towards authority figures. In fact, Paul speaks about one of the core principles surrounding it in one of his letters:

*Everyone must submit himself to the governing authorities, for there is no authority except that which God has established. The authorities that exist have been established by God. Consequently, he who rebels against the authority is rebelling against what God has instituted …*

(Romans 13:1–2a)

This of course raises questions for all of us as to what we should do in certain situations. For example, what should our response be if something that an authority figure asks us to do goes against other core spiritual principles, or if that individual is abusive towards us? These are not easy questions to answer as there are a number of factors involved, but the key to understanding the issues is to do with our heart attitude. Sometimes we need to separate our heart attitude[23] from what is being asked of us. To put it another way, submission does not necessarily mean complete obedience to an authority figure as it is an attitude rather than an action.

In Vashti's case there does not seem to have been any circumstances that warranted her behaviour. In fact, we are told that:

*Memucan replied in the presence of the king and the nobles, 'Queen Vashti has done wrong, not only against the king but also against all the nobles and the peoples of all the provinces of King Xerxes.'*

(Esther 1:16)

Sometimes, as was clearly the case with Vashti, refusing to do something that an authority figure requires us to do may have a much wider impact on others than perhaps we are aware of at the time. For this reason, we need to be particularly careful how we respond in such challenging situations.

Having said that, in situations where there has been any kind of abuse it is vital for us to take whatever seems to be the obvious action. But if there are circumstances involving someone else, and we feel unsure about the route God wants us to take out of the situation, we need to be more cautious. We should pray about it, then wait until God shows us what we should do. Once we know what God is saying to us, we then need to talk to the Holy Spirit and ask Him to partner with us in whatever action we have to take.

Memucan goes on to say that:

> *the queen's conduct will become known to all the women, and so they will despise their husbands and say, 'King Xerxes commanded Queen Vashti to be brought before him, but she would not come.'*
>
> (Esther 1:17)

Memucan's concern that other women would follow Vashti's example was a very real possibility and needs to be recognised as such. Looking at society in our own time, and the way in which certain popular people in the media are followed by others, we can see the reality of his concern. Our example needs to be Jesus Himself; otherwise we can find ourselves in a situation where we suddenly realise that we have given someone else His place in our hearts. This is of course idolatry. Such situations are very damaging as eventually that person says or does something that hurts us badly and acts as a wake-up call. I went through a situation of this kind a few years ago. The person in question was someone who showed me such kindness that I opened my heart to them. This person then broke the trust I had put in them, which wounded me deeply. In fact, the wounding was so deep that it took me rather a long time to work through with God. Even now I still occasionally have moments of grief about all that happened.

Having restated his view of the situation, Memucan then goes on to say that Vashti should be banished from the king's presence and another queen should be found to replace her.[24] Suggesting that Vashti should be banished from the king's presence might seem rather harsh by today's standards, but, as will be seen from an event later in the book, her punishment could have been a lot worse; things were done very differently in that era. There is apparently no historical record of exactly what happened to Queen Vashti, but the most likely explanation is that she lived out the rest of her life in seclusion somewhere in the palace grounds.

Memucan's recommendation was accepted by Xerxes and his nobles.[25] They also decided that dispatches should be sent out:

> *to all parts of the kingdom, to each province in its own script and to each people in its own language, proclaiming in each people's tongue that every man should be ruler over his own household.*
>
> (Esther 1:22)

Initially it seems as if what is said here about husbands is the same thing that Paul says in Ephesians 5:22–23 – that a wife must submit to her husband and that the husband is the head of the wife. However, reading on a bit further in Ephesians, it soon becomes apparent that that is just not the case:

> *Husbands, love your wives, just as Christ loved the church and gave himself up for her …*
> (Ephesians 5:25)

This tells us that the decree of King Xerxes is not based on God's vision for marriage, because the sacrificial nature of the love shown by Christ towards His Church had not been demonstrated in that earlier time. This of course means it would not have been the basis of the model used for marriages then. In fact, since ancient Persia was a very patriarchal society, and women were therefore considered to be property, their model of marriage would not have been anything like the kind of marriage portrayed by Paul in Ephesians; women generally would have had little say in things.

We can also see, if we continue reading Paul's words in Ephesians 5, that the marriage between a man and a woman is clearly linked to the marriage between Christ and the Church. Jesus 'gave himself up for her':

*to make her holy, cleansing her by the washing with water through the word, and to present her to himself as a radiant church, without stain or wrinkle or any other blemish, but holy and blameless.*
(Ephesians 5:26–27)

From this passage, then, we learn something about God's heart for the Church as a whole and His plans for us in the future. Moreover, further on in the same chapter we are told that the relationship between Christ and the Church is a 'mystery'.[26] This means that we only see, and live in, a small part of God's full revelation; we only know what that looks like for the moment. However, once we join Him in glory, we will live in and experience the full revelation of what the Church truly looks like from Heaven's perspective.

# ENDNOTE REFERENCES

1    ESTHER 1:4–7
2    JOHN 2:1–11
3    ESTHER 1:9
4    REVELATION 19:9
5    REVELATION 19:11–16
6    1 THESSALONIANS 4:16–17
7    REVELATION 19:9
8    ESTHER 1:12
9    1 JOHN 1:8–9
10   MATTHEW 16:24–25
11   REVELATION 12:7–9
12   ISAIAH 14:12–15; EZEKIEL 28:12–19
13   JOHN 13:12–17
14   2 CORINTHIANS 3:18
15   ROMANS 12:9–16
16   JOHN 16:8–11
17   JOHN 16:13
18   ROMANS 12:2
19   JEREMIAH 29:11
20   ESTHER 1:12–14
21   EPHESIANS 4:26–27
22   PROVERBS 15:22
23   1 SAMUEL 16:7B
24   ESTHER 1:18–20
25   ESTHER 1:21
26   EPHESIANS 5:32

*her with her beauty treatments and special food. He assigned to*
*her seven maids selected from the king's palace and moved her and*
*her maids into the best place in the harem.*

(Esther 2:9)

What was it about Esther that won Hegai's favour and caused him to give her special treatment? Obviously, there was something about her that made her stand out from the crowd. It seems probable that Hegai saw something different in her attitude and behaviour compared to the other girls. Perhaps the way in which she was handling the situation caused Hegai to think she had the potential to be a good queen, hence the preferential treatment that he gave her.

As Christians we should stand out from the crowd too; our attitudes and behaviour, in fact our whole way of life, should be such that people ask us what is different about us. However, we live in a time when all too many of the lines have become blurred within church life, and some believers do not seem to recognise the need to live as differently from those around them as once was the case. This means that all too often people outside the Church are not able to see much difference between someone who is a professing Christian and someone who is not, which of course can have a negative impact on our witness, both individually and corporately.

Perhaps we need to remind ourselves, and each other, from time to time that in 1 John 2:15–17 Scripture says:

*Do not love the world or anything in the world. If anyone loves*
*the world, the love of the Father is not in him. For everything in*
*the world – the cravings of sinful man, the lust of his eyes and the*

*boasting of what he has and does – comes not from the Father but from the world. The world and its desires pass away, but the man who does the will of God lives for ever.*

This passage should give us the desire to look more carefully at our attitudes and behaviour, particularly if we are reading and meditating on God's Word regularly, because that is the plumb line of truth.[5] However, it is important for us all to remember that trying to bring about change in any area of our lives in our own strength will be self-defeating – and even soul-destroying. When we recognise that we need to change in some way, we need to ask the Holy Spirit to help us. He is more than willing to enable us to change in whatever way is necessary since doing so is part of His role in our lives.[6]

Another thing that might have marked Esther out as being different was her upbringing; things that are said about Mordecai further on in the book indicate that he was a believer, and that means he would have brought Esther up to be the same. Hegai would not have known this at this point in the story because Mordecai had forbidden Esther to speak about her nationality and family background[7] – undoubtedly because of the high levels of persecution that Jewish people faced in the region at that time. Throughout history, the people of God have been persecuted for their faith, sometimes more obviously than at other times. This is important to be aware of because, whilst we should never expect persecution, we need to recognise that it is not abnormal for believers to be persecuted[8] and therefore we should not condemn those to whom this has happened, or is happening.

Sadly, the way in which Hegai singled Esther out would have

resulted in at least some of the other girls becoming jealous of her. Those girls would have been rather spiteful towards her, so it is probable that at times life was more difficult for Esther in the harem than it was for the others. Like anger, jealousy can be very destructive and damaging, so when we recognise that we have a problem in this area, we need to work through the issues involved in partnership with the Holy Spirit as soon as we can, preferably before it leads us into doing something we will later come to regret.

Of course emotions in themselves are not necessarily wrong; however, if not handled well, they can lead to us behaving, or acting, in ways that are. Furthermore, we must learn how to deal with them appropriately, as doing so is a sign of maturity, both as a person and as a Christian.

Going back to the story, we now read that:

*Before a girl's turn came to go in to King Xerxes, she had to complete twelve months of beauty treatments prescribed for the women, six months with oil of myrrh and six with perfumes and cosmetics.*
(Esther 2:12)

The oil of myrrh is derived from a bitter herb and is an astringent, which means that it constricts the soft tissues of the human body, restricting the flow of bodily fluids. It was used in the anointing oil in the Temple, and also in the oil that was used to create the incense for it. These two preparations were meant for God alone and were not to be used outside of the Temple; if anyone was found doing so they could face the death penalty.

Moreover, myrrh was one of the gifts given to Jesus by the

wise men when He was born,[9] He was anointed with it twice by two different women at different points in His life,[10] and it was used as part of the preparation for His burial.[11] Not only that; Jesus was offered it to drink after He had been nailed to the cross, although He refused it.[12]

Studying the various references to myrrh in the life of Jesus, as well as the others that are scattered throughout the Bible, soon reveals that it speaks of cleansing and purification, and of repentance and being set apart for God. For us it therefore represents aspects of the journey of transformation that we are all undergoing in order to prepare us to be part of the company of people that will ultimately become the Bride of Christ.

The same kind of thing applied to Esther during her first six months in the harem, except that she was being prepared to enter the presence of an earthly king, Xerxes. But just as is the case for us, that was not all that was involved in her preparation. Whilst she would have smelt of myrrh and her skin would have been greatly softened at the end of that period more was still needed. Esther needed to smell of the kind of fragrance that would please her king, and the same applies to us regarding our Heavenly King. This happens as we progressively live lives that reflect the worship that is in our hearts to those around us by living to please Him, rather than ourselves.[13] The more we live this way, the stronger our 'heavenly fragrance' will be and the more it will impact the lives of others. Scripture says this will happen in one of two ways:

*For we are to God the aroma of Christ among those who are being saved and those who are perishing. To the one we are the smell of death; to the other, the fragrance of life.* (2 Corinthians 2:15–16)

This, incidentally, can be the reason why some people react to us negatively without speaking to us, or even knowing us, so if you get an odd response from someone who is a stranger to you, forgive the person in question and pray for their salvation!

Continuing with the Esther story, we read:

*And this is how [a girl] would go to the king: Anything she wanted was given to her to take with her from the harem to the king's palace. In the evening she would go there and in the morning return to another part of the harem to the care of Shaashgaz, the king's eunuch who was in charge of the concubines. She would not return to the king unless he was pleased with her and summoned her by name.*

(Esther 2:13–14)

We are told that when the girls were going in to see the king, they were given the chance to choose whatever clothes and jewellery they wanted for what might be their only night with him. In all probability most of them grabbed the chance to take whatever they could, whether they needed it or not, possibly even if it did not suit them. This is because they knew that if they were not called back in to see the king again, whatever they took with them was all they would have to make a comfortable future for themselves; so undoubtedly the majority of them would have taken full advantage of the opportunity they had been given.

Esther, however, did not do this kind of thing when her time came to go to the king.[14] We are told that she in fact:

*asked for nothing other than what Hegai, the king's eunuch who was in charge of the harem, suggested. And Esther won the favour of everyone who saw her.* (Esther 2:15)

At this point there is a rather important question: How did Esther with her background reconcile herself to experiencing the intimacy of the bedroom without being at least betrothed to the man she was going to be with? Since she had been brought up in the household of someone who knew the Lord, it seems probable that Esther too was a believer and that she must have at some point decided to surrender the situation to God because she was powerless to change it. Only He would be able to work things out in her favour.

So often, it is only when we find our lives are beyond our control, as Esther would have done, that we yield ourselves to the Lord; all too often there is a part of us that wants to do things our own way rather than the way God wants. However, deep inside of us is the knowledge that God is the only one who can do anything about the situation we are facing, and that since we have reached the end of ourselves, we have no choice but to trust Him. Obviously, this is not usually something we end up doing just once, and each time we do it our dependency on God deepens and thus our faith increases.

The story of Shadrach, Meshach and Abednego, who were thrown into a fiery furnace, illustrates perfectly not only their dependence on God, but also their willingness to surrender the consequences of their actions to Him.[15] The king of Persia at the time, Nebuchadnezzar, set up an idol that his people were expected to worship whenever they heard music playing. Shadrach, Meshach and Abednego refused to do this and were reported to Nebuchadnezzar. When the men were challenged

# 3

# ESTHER IS MADE QUEEN

*Now the king was attracted to Esther more than to any of the other women, and she won his favour and approval more than any of the other virgins. So he set a royal crown on her head and made her queen instead of Vashti. And the king gave a great banquet, Esther's banquet, for all his nobles and officials. He proclaimed a holiday throughout the provinces and distributed gifts with royal liberality.*

(Esther 2:17–18)

What did Xerxes like about Esther so much that he wanted her to be his queen? To have her crowned queen after having only spent one night with her shows us that he must have seen something in her that made her stand out from the other girls. Had Hegai perhaps already given Xerxes a favourable report about Esther's attitude and behaviour whilst she was in the harem? This is a strong possibility, as it seems unlikely that Xerxes would see the girls without first being told something about them by Hegai.

Over the years I have realised that what we say when we speak about others can reveal more about us than whatever we say about ourselves. This is because, when we have been hurt badly by someone, we can become rather judgmental in the way we speak about that person,[1] and about others too. We can show people something of what is going on in our heart and, if that is not right, they themselves may treat us badly – even if what we are saying about the other person is true. When we release the person who hurt us from what they did to us,[2] we also need to let go of any judgements that we have made about them because that is what true forgiveness entails[3]. This means that we are then in the right place to receive the healing that we need, and also to talk, if necessary, about what happened with the right attitude. However, it took me many years – and a lot of pain – to reach this understanding.

The actions that Xerxes took to celebrate making Esther his queen also show us that she must have made quite an impact on his heart. Did Xerxes perhaps fall in love with Esther during their night together? It seems probable, particularly in the light of what happens later on in the story, but we cannot say for certain as the Bible is silent on this subject, just as it is with regard to Esther's feelings about all that happened to her. We may not know for certain how Xerxes, or Esther, felt, but God did. Moreover, since He is omniscient (all-knowing), He knows how each one of us feels about the things that are happening in our lives. The Psalms show us clearly that we can go to God with our feelings, and they also reveal something of the way in which He helps us to work them through as we spend time worshipping Him.[4] This is because God longs to have an intimate relationship with each one of us, just as we do with

Him, and the basis for such a relationship with anyone is the sharing of hearts and lives.

Shortly after the passage about the king's decision to make Esther queen, we are told once again that:

> *Esther had kept secret her family background and nationality just as Mordecai had told her to do, for she continued to follow Mordecai's instructions as she had done when he was bringing her up.*
>
> (Esther 2:20)

The emphasis in this verse on Esther's relationship with Mordecai is another indication of its importance, particularly in terms of this story. This comes through again in the incident that follows, but before we look at that, it is important to make a mental note of the fact that Esther was still being mentored by Mordecai and taking his advice; this will help us to have a good understanding of later events.

We are told that when Mordecai was 'sitting at the king's gate' he overheard two of the guards conspiring to kill Xerxes and that he spoke to Esther about it. She then told the king, who had the men investigated. When it was established that what Mordecai had told Esther was true, the two men were executed and a written record was made of the incident.[5]

The significance of the incident just described will be seen more clearly later in the story, but it is important to recognise that Mordecai was not angry, resentful or bitter by this time about the way in which he had been previously treated;[6] otherwise he would not have passed on what he heard. In fact, this is a clear indication that he had put his faith in God. It is highly unlikely that Mordecai would have been able to forgive those who had massacred his people and taken him into exile if he had not experienced God's forgiveness himself. In other words, the fact that Mordecai reported the two guards shows us that he must have worked through with God the issues of his past. If we leave the things that have happened to us in our past unresolved, we can end up being held in captivity to it, but working things through with God and forgiving those who have hurt us will set us free to enter our 'promised land'.

We now meet a new character in the story:

*After these events, King Xerxes honoured Haman son of Hamme-datha, the Agagite, elevating him and giving him a seat of honour higher than that of all the other nobles.*

(Esther 3:1)

It is worth noting at this point that Haman was an Agagite, which means that he was a descendant of Agag, the king of the Amalekites at the time of the exodus from Egypt. This is significant, not only because of the way in which his people attacked the Israelites shortly after their escape from Egypt,[7] but also because of their later history,[8] which we will now briefly look at for reasons that will become apparent further on in the chapter.

The first king of Israel, Saul, was told by Samuel, the prophet, that God wanted him to take his army and destroy the Amalekites completely. However, the Biblical account makes it clear that King Saul did not do exactly what God asked of him. The result of this is obvious, since we are told that Haman was related to Agag, which tells us that some of the Amalekites got away. Later in the book we will see just how costly Saul's disobedience could have been to the Jewish people.

The verse that follows says:

*All the royal officials at the king's gate knelt down and paid honour to Haman, for the king had commanded this concerning him. But Mordecai would not kneel down or pay him honour.*

(Esther 3:2)

These royal officials probably felt obliged to give homage to Haman. However, the Bible clearly teaches us that honour is not something that should be demanded; it is a matter of personal choice.

True honour flows out of experiencing the unconditional love of God and living in a way that reflects that in our lives. This is because, as we progressively incarnate the love and the character of Christ in our lives,[9] we will increasingly want to do what we have been asked to do and will then willingly honour others above ourselves.[10] We will also want to honour those in authority over us in whatever way is appropriate, as we recognise that by doing so we are demonstrating our love for God.[11]

According to Jesus, honour is not something we should seek for ourselves. This can be seen from these words, spoken by Jesus Himself:

*whoever exalts himself will be humbled, and whoever humbles himself will be exalted.*

(Matthew 23:12)

However, this principle is encapsulated not just in some of Jesus' teaching, but also in the way He lived out His life. Out of all this we can see that humility results in honour.[12]

Mordecai seems to have been the only one who did not want to honour Haman in the way that he thought he was entitled to. Since we are not told the reason for Mordecai's behaviour, here are three possibilities that are worth consideration:

1. Were there perhaps unresolved issues between Mordecai and Haman prior to this?

2. Did Mordecai feel that Haman wanted people to bow down to him in a way that we should only do for God, rather than in a manner appropriate for another human being in authority?

3. Was he acting in obedience to God in behaving in the way that he did?

The third seems to be the most likely explanation.

We are now told what happened as a result:

*the royal officials at the king's gate asked Mordecai, 'Why do you disobey the king's command?' Day after day they spoke to him but he refused to comply. Therefore they told Haman about it to see whether Mordecai's behaviour would be tolerated, for he had told them he was a Jew.* (Esther 3:3–4)

As we have just seen, the reason for Mordecai's refusal to obey the king's command is not clearly stated in Scripture; neither is it clear why he goes on refusing to do so. Mordecai's action is particularly significant since he would have known the kind of punishment that awaited someone who was disobedient in this way, so he must have had a good reason for behaving as he did. It looks as if he wanted to make a point and yet we are not told in Scripture exactly what that was.

This may of course suggest that his disobedience to Xerxes' command was an act of obedience to God. It is also possible that the writer of Esther assumed that those reading the book would understand the reason for Mordecai's disobedience. Alternatively, perhaps the writer did not want the focus taken away from the main thrust of the story, which is not primarily about Mordecai but about the power of a life given to God and His purposes.

Whatever the case:

> *When Haman saw that Mordecai would not kneel down or pay him honour, he was enraged. Yet having learned who Mordecai's people were, he scorned the idea of killing only Mordecai. Instead Haman looked for a way to destroy all Mordecai's people, the Jews, throughout the whole kingdom of Xerxes.* (Esther 3:5–6)

Haman's response goes far beyond what most people would see as reasonable, just or even fair in such situations. In fact, it became an act of hatred and revenge. It seems probable that his attitude was not just about a refusal to honour him, but also the result of a deep-seated hatred of the Jews instilled in him when he was growing up. This would have arisen because of the history, discussed earlier, between the Jews and his people.

Such an attitude runs completely counter to the way in which we as Christians are called to deal with such situations.[13] In fact, Jesus told His disciples:

> *Love your enemies, do good to those who hate you, bless those who curse you, pray for those who ill-treat you … Do to others as you would have them do to you.*

> (Luke 6:27–28, 31)

To live like this is completely countercultural, costly and virtually impossible for us to do in our own strength. However, that in a sense is the point, as it is only in partnership with the Holy Spirit that we can live the way that Jesus calls us to and thus discover God's heart for us. At its core, true faith is not just about trusting God, but living in dependence on Him,[14] and once we begin to live like this we are on our way to becoming the mature 'sons', described as 'fathers', in 1 John 2:12–14. (Note: Our 'sonship' has nothing to do with gender, but is about relationship and inheritance.)

Going back to the Esther story, the next thing that happens is the casting of a kind of lot, known as a *pur*, for the purpose of setting a date for Haman's revenge on the Jews. This was done by some of the royal officials in Haman's presence. The lot fell on the twelfth day of Adar, which is the twelfth month of the year.[15]

The *pur* was a set of dice that was used in the first month of a year in the Persian court to establish propitious dates for the various events planned for that year. This was an indication of the Persians' belief in fate: good and bad omens were the deciding factor in when, or whether, action should be taken. Obviously, any activity of this kind is not something that we as Christians should indulge in. Such activities are not just wrong[16] but will also open a door into our lives that the enemy can, and will, take advantage of at some point.

We read on:

*Then Haman said to King Xerxes, 'There is a certain people dispersed and scattered among the peoples in all the provinces of your kingdom whose customs are different from those of all other*

56

*people and who do not obey the king's laws; it is not in the king's best interest to tolerate them.'*

(Esther 3:8)

Haman now manipulates Xerxes into doing exactly what he wants by not only *not* specifying the ethnicity of the people he is talking about, but also cleverly suggesting that these people pose a risk to the king and his kingdom. Moreover, Haman goes on to suggest the making of a decree to destroy them and offers Xerxes a rather large sum of money to sweeten the pot. Xerxes refused the bribe, but willingly gave Haman the freedom to write the necessary decree that would fulfil Haman's desire to bring about the destruction of the Jews living in the empire.[17]

From what is said it seems as if Xerxes did not question whether what Haman told him was true or not, which suggests that he had put a high level of trust in Haman's judgement and perspective. Generally, a good leader will ask questions and establish the truth of a situation before taking whatever action may be needed. However, Xerxes did not do so. He may of course have been preoccupied with other matters of state or family. This is a reasonable explanation because, whilst he is generally considered to have been on the harsh side as a ruler, and something of a failure as a military leader, his statesmanship was not especially poor.

As Christians, most of us are aware that we are in the middle of a war and that:

*our struggle is not against flesh and blood, but against the rulers, against the authorities, against the powers of this dark world and against the spiritual forces of evil in the heavenly realms.*

(Ephesians 6:12)

The war that we are talking about is between good and evil, the Kingdom of Light and the kingdom of darkness, and is something we cannot afford to ignore. To do so will be very costly in the long run.

Moreover, just as Hegai can be viewed as being a picture, a type, of the Holy Spirit, Haman can be seen as representing our enemy, the devil, who is described as a murderer and a liar from the beginning.[18] This means that Esther's story has a lot to teach us about overcoming the enemy's power in our lives.

For now, we need to remind ourselves that one of the greatest keys to being an overcomer is in understanding that God's desire for us to live holy lives[19] is primarily for our own well-being and protection. Moreover, it is important to recognise that holiness is not just about *not* doing the things that God considers to be wrong; that is only one aspect of it. Holiness is also about discovering the richness of living in a way that pleases God – about being set free from the things that hold us in bondage, finding the path to wholeness and discovering God's heart for us. Most importantly of all, it is about discovering who God is, because doing so will enable us to become more and more intimate with Him.[20]

Returning to the story:

*Then on the thirteenth day of the first month the royal secretaries were summoned. They wrote out in the script of each province and in the language of each people all Haman's orders to the king's satraps, the governors of the various provinces and the nobles of the various peoples. These were written in the name of King Xerxes himself and sealed with his own ring.* (Esther 3:12)

When an authority figure delegates some of their authority to someone else, they need to also put in place an accountability structure of some kind, not only for the protection of those under their authority but also for their own protection. For example: If a church leader appoints an associate pastor, it might be a good idea for them to have regular meetings with that person to discuss and pray about the various people and things they are involved with. Not only that; there should be a robust process for dealing with any issues people have with them. This should be based on Matthew 18:15–17 and it needs to have been properly explained to the congregation, not just put on a noticeboard somewhere, or even the church website, under some obscure heading. Finally, and most importantly, the senior leader needs to schedule time in his or her diary to talk and listen to God about the associate and their work for the Kingdom, not just when an issue arises but on a regular basis.

Going on from the previous verse, we read that:

*Dispatches were sent by couriers to all the king's provinces with the order to destroy, kill and annihilate all the Jews – young and old, women and little children – on a single day, the thirteenth day of the twelfth month, the month of Adar, and to plunder their goods.* (Esther 3:13)

The way in which these dispatches were written clearly reveals to us the depth of Haman's hatred for the Jews, and we need to recognise that our enemy feels much the same way about us. This is the reason why it is so important for us to resist the temptation to live in the same way as those who do not know God,[21] or to put it another way, to live holy lives. If we do not do so, we risk opening ourselves up to being attacked in some way, as our enemy is always on the lookout for opportunities to harm us.[22]

The date set for Haman's plan to be enacted was the day before Passover and that cannot be just a coincidence. It once again points to the enemy's hatred for the people of God, because that feast marked the Israelites' escape from the land of slavery[23] and the start of their journey into the promised land. For us, as Christians, Passover speaks of Jesus being the Lamb of God[24] and of the need to apply His blood to our lives.[25] It is as we do this that our journey out of the bondage of sin onto the path of salvation begins. This is the first step towards beginning to discover God's heart for us as individuals.

The closing verses of the third chapter of Esther reiterate details of the distribution of the edict. They also speak of the confusion of the citizens of Susa when they hear of it,[26] something that indicates that they did not understand the reason behind the proposed annihilation of the Jews. This strongly suggests that the Jewish people had followed Jeremiah's advice to them when they were exiled and had been building new lives for themselves until it was time for the promised return to their land.[27]

# ENDNOTE REFERENCES

1       LUKE 6:37–38
2       MATTHEW 18:21–35
3       MATTHEW 18:21–35
4       PSALM 28:1–9
5       ESTHER 2:21–23
6       ESTHER 2:5–6
7       EXODUS 17:8–16
8       1 SAMUEL 15:1–33
9       GALATIANS 3:26; 5:22–25
10      ROMANS 12:10B
11      ROMANS 13:7
12      PHILIPPIANS 2:5–11; NOTE ESPECIALLY VERSE 9.
13      ROMANS 12:17–21
14      ROMANS 8:14
15      ESTHER 3:7
16      DEUTERONOMY 18:10–12: LEVITICUS 19:31
17      ESTHER 3:10–11
18      JOHN 8:44
19      1 THESSALONIANS 4:7–8
20      HEBREWS 12:14
21      ROMANS 12:2
22      1 PETER 5:8
23      EXODUS 12:21–28
24      JOHN 1:29
25      EXODUS 12:21–23
26      ESTHER 3:14–15
27      JEREMIAH 29:1–23

# 4

# MORDECAI AND THE FIRST EDICT

*When Mordecai learned of all that had been done, he tore his clothes, put on sackcloth and ashes, and went out into the city, wailing loudly and bitterly. But he went only as far as the king's gate, because no-one clothed in sackcloth was allowed to enter it. In every province to which the edict and order of the king came, there was great mourning among the Jews, with fasting, weeping and wailing. Many lay in sackcloth and ashes.*

(Esther 4:1–3)

M ordecai's response to the edict, described in the above verses, is another indication of his faith in God, because in the Old Testament era sackcloth and ashes speak of debasement, mourning and repentance. Such behaviour is therefore an act of humility, which in Mordecai's case indicated that he was interceding for his people in a way that today is sometimes referred to as 'identificational repentance'.[1] As the quotation also shows, Mordecai was not the only one to respond in this way: there were many more Jews praying for God's intervention on behalf of their people.

Developing good communication with someone is essential if we want to build a healthy relationship with them, and that applies just as much to our relationship with God as it does to our human relationships. Just as there are a wide variety of ways for us to communicate with each other, so the same is true regarding our relationship with God. Spending time alone with God is the biggest key to developing our relationship with Him, but there are other things that will be of value in that process. Whilst to a large extent prayer is more 'caught than taught', studying what the Bible has to say on the subject can open our eyes to the range of different ways that we can communicate with God and He with us – as of course can good teaching about it. The Bible also teaches us about the nature and character of God and the principles of His Kingdom. This can enable us to build a more intimate relationship with Him, because the more we understand about a person, the easier it is to relate to them.

Esther heard about the way in which Mordecai was behaving and was extremely distressed about it because she did not know what was behind it. Initially she sent Mordecai some clothing, but when he refused her gift she asked Hathach, one of the eunuchs assigned to her, to go and ask him what was going on:[2]

*So Hathach went out to Mordecai in the open square of the city in front of the king's gate. Mordecai told him everything that had happened to him, including the exact amount of money Haman had promised to pay into the royal treasury for the destruction of the Jews.*

(Esther 4:6–7)

Mordecai was very open with Hathach, which may have been due to the gravity of the situation and the trust that had been placed in him by Esther. It does, however, raise the question of how well the men knew each other prior to this situation, because generally the kind of openness indicated in these verses takes time to develop; but the Bible does not tell us. Not only that; the openness between the two men can be seen as a picture of the truth[3] and honesty[4] that God wants us to have in our relationships with one another. Obviously, for those of us who have a problem with trust this may be something of an issue, but it is important to remember that God is always willing to heal us from the root of such things.

When the two men had finished speaking, Mordecai gave Hathach a copy of the edict for him to give to Esther, along with a request that she should speak to the king and ask for his mercy for her people.[5] However, Esther sent Hathach back to Mordecai to explain that the restrictions upon her because of royal protocol meant she would not be able to fulfil his request:

*All the king's officials and the people of the royal provinces know that for any man or woman who approaches the king in the inner court without being summoned the king has but one law: that he be put to death.*

(Esther 4:10a)

Every palace has its protocol, just as every executive residence has its formal rules of conduct, and anyone who visits such places needs to have some understanding of what is involved. The greater, or higher, the person whose residence is being visited, the more detailed and rigid the protocol is likely to be. Since King Xerxes was the richest and most powerful monarch of his time, the protocol in his palace was very formal and rigid. Not only that; there had been a history of previous monarchs being killed by family members, or trusted advisers, so the security was very tight for his own protection. This of course added to the protocol of his court, making it even more unwieldy than it would have otherwise been.

For us too there is a kind of protocol that comes into play at times in our relationship with God. This is because, although as His children we can generally just enter His presence whenever we want to, there are times, and perhaps even seasons, when a different approach is needed. Such an approach will be more formal in nature as we will not be coming to God as one of His children but as a citizen of heaven. We will briefly look at one such situation in Chapter Six. Perhaps here I should say that whilst she broke with the protocol of the court in doing so she does give us a guide to the protocol of heaven for our times of intercession.

Continuing to explain the death sentence for someone approaching the king unbidden, Hathach goes on to say:

*The only exception to this is for the king to extend the gold sceptre to him and spare his life. But thirty days have passed since I was called to go to the king.* (Esther 4:10b)

This part of the story echoes something of the way in which the high priest could only enter the 'most holy place' in the Tabernacle or Temple once a year, on what is known as the Day of Atonement.[6] This was because he could only do so after making certain preparations, without which his life might be at risk.[7]

Within Judaism there is a tradition that describes one of the things that had to be done prior to the high priest going into the most holy place: a rope was tied around his ankle so that if he died whilst he was in the 'holy of holies' he could be pulled out by it. This of course meant that no one else had to go in there to bring him out. Whilst most theologians think it is unlikely that this ever really happened, it does give us a certain amount of insight into how Jewish religious leaders understood the holiness of God. Passages such as Leviticus 10:1–4 and Exodus 7:1–26 give us further understanding of how they might have seen God's holiness, which for us is just one aspect of the progressive revelation of the character and nature of God given by the Bible.

In other words, whilst the God that we worship is primarily a God of love, as has been said previously, He is also holy. For us to be able to become more intimate with God, we need to keep on asking the Holy Spirit to partner with us in dealing with any issues that would prevent us from experiencing the greater intimacy that we are seeking with Him. This means learning to recognise the promptings that the Holy Spirit will give us about the areas of our lives that need to change and responding to them in whatever way is appropriate.[8]

The answer that Esther gives to Mordecai shows us that she is understandably concerned about the risk involved for her if she takes any action that does not follow the protocol of the palace. In fact, Esther basically says that if she does what he asks her to do, it will probably result in her death. And yet:

*When Esther's words were reported to Mordecai, he sent back this answer: 'Do not think that because you are in the king's house you alone of all the Jews will escape. For if you remain silent at this time, relief and deliverance for the Jews will arise from another place, but you and your father's family will perish. And who knows but that you have come to royal position for such a time as this?'*

(Esther 4:12–14)

Asking someone to be willing to sacrifice their life for others is rather a lot to ask of them and yet people are asked to do this in defence of their country on a regular basis. However, history shows us that there many people who are willing to make sacrifices, including giving up their own lives, if they believe that the reason is good enough and that their sacrifice is going to save lives. Of course this brings me to Jesus, who willingly laid down His life to purchase our salvation.[9]

Esther faced an impossible choice, as most of us probably have at some point in our lives – although perhaps not in such a life-and-death situation. Mordecai's challenge to Esther may well be the kind of challenge that some of us will face in some way, because our circumstances may mean taking a risk that if unsuccessful might be very costly to us, or to people we care about. It is therefore vital for us to remember that 'Faith is spelt R-I-S-K', as John Wimber used to say, recognising that if what we are considering doing is in obedience to God then the outcome is entirely in His hands. Even when we get things wrong, the principle spoken of in Romans 8:28–30 still applies

– that God always works for the good of those who love him. This means that although we may have made what is in some way a costly mistake, in another sense we will not miss out as God will use whatever has happened for our good.

One of the best Biblical stories to illustrate this principle from Romans is that of Joseph, who was sold into slavery by his brothers.[10] A few years later he was put in prison for purportedly trying to rape his master's wife.[11] Whilst Joseph was in prison, he met two men and interpreted their dreams for them.[12] When one of the men, the pharaoh's cupbearer, was restored to his position in just the way that Joseph had predicted from his dream, the man promised to speak to Pharaoh about him – but forgot.[13] However, when Pharaoh later had a couple of dreams that no one else could interpret, the cupbearer remembered Joseph and told Pharaoh about the way in which he had correctly interpreted his dream.[14]

This resulted in Joseph being brought to the palace by Pharaoh to interpret his dreams. Joseph explained to Pharaoh that his dreams foretold a terrible famine, and the advice that he gave about dealing with this disaster caused him to be swiftly promoted from the prison to the palace.[15] Joseph's position as second only to Pharaoh meant that when his family came to Egypt to buy food during the famine, he was positioned to be able to help them. To cut a long story short, Joseph arranged for the whole family to move to Egypt.[16]

The story of Joseph is a remarkable one and the outline just given of it does not really do it justice, but the point is to enable you to understand this remark made by Joseph to his brothers after his father's death when they were obviously bothered about their future:

*You intended to harm me, but God intended it for good to accomplish what is now being done, the saving of many lives.*

(Genesis 50:20)

Through the story of Joseph, we can see that God can turn something that was intended for evil into something that would bring about His purposes for the people involved. In the story of Esther we will shortly see that same spiritual principle at work in her too. Moreover, we may see this principle at work in our own lives and the lives of those around us.

Mordecai's comment about Esther, namely that she was in the position she was in 'for such a time as this', has been used to speak into issues such as free will and predestination. For the purposes of this book a slightly less theological approach is more appropriate, but having said that, when we look at Mordecai's words in the context of the book of Esther as a whole, the sentence is without a shadow of a doubt prophetic in nature. In fact, it is the key to unlocking some of the truths hidden in this exceptional book as it speaks into the way in which God has a purpose for each of our lives.[17]

As Christians it is vital for us to have some understanding of the nature of 'the prophetic', as we are all to some degree and in some way prophetic. However, this does not necessarily mean that we will operate in the gift of prophecy[18] or be set into the office of a prophet.[19]

Perhaps here a simple explanation is needed, particularly for those who are yet unfamiliar with the term 'prophetic'. It is a word that describes certain ways and forms that God uses to communicate with His people. It includes what the Bible calls a 'word of knowledge' or a 'word of wisdom', as well as prophecies.

It can come in many forms – words, pictures, dreams and visions being the most common. The passage that follows gives us an example of the kind of thing we are speaking about:

*During the night Paul had a vision of a man of Macedonia standing and begging him, 'Come over to Macedonia and help us.' After Paul had seen the vision, we got ready at once to leave for Macedonia, concluding that God had called us to preach the gospel to them.*

(Acts 16:9–10)

Just as Paul and those with him at the time he had the dream responded and took what seemed to be the required action, we need to learn to do the same when God speaks to us. If God speaks to us and we are not sure what we should do next, then we probably need to seek Him for further clarification ourselves before speaking to anyone else about what our next step should be. This is because if we speak to too many people or, for that matter, to the wrong people, the waters can get very muddy to say the least – as I know from personal experience!

Esther's response to Mordecai after his message was to ask him to ask all the Jews living in the city to fast with her and her maids for three days prior to her seeking an audience with the king.[20] Her willingness to lay her life down for her people shows us to whom her heart truly belonged. In that moment Esther is a prophetic picture of what Jesus would later physically do to purchase our salvation.[21]

Esther would have been familiar with the following verse from the book of Isaiah. It connects fasting with injustice, and it may well have been part of the reason behind the fast that she embarked on:

*Is not this the kind of fasting I have chosen: to loose the chains of injustice and untie the cords of the yoke, to set the oppressed free and break every yoke?*

(Isaiah 58:6)

Jesus fasted,[22] and we will be called upon by the Holy Spirit to do likewise from time to time.[23] When used appropriately, fasting can help to bring about amazing breakthroughs, not just in our lives and the lives of those around us, but also in our nation. However, if we have major health issues we may need to discuss our desire to fast with a medical professional, because in such a situation it may be detrimental to our health to abstain completely from food.

The Jews involved in the fast would have understood that there is no point in fasting without praying. Those three days would have involved not just intercession but also a lot of heart searching, because we cannot intercede effectively for anyone if our heart is not right before the Lord.[24] This means that there would have been a lot of personal repentance; so often, this is what brings the breakthrough that is being sought.

For us it also means asking our guide, the Holy Spirit, to show us not just what to pray for, but how to do so, as sometimes the obvious way to pray will not achieve the kind of outcome we are longing for. We then need to wait until we have heard whatever He has to say to us[25] before we start to pray into the situation and seek a breakthrough in it.

Going back to the story again, we read that:

*On the third day Esther put on her royal robes and stood in the inner court of the palace, in front of the king's hall. The king was*

*sitting on his royal throne in the hall, facing the entrance. When he*
*saw Queen Esther standing in the court, he was pleased with her*
*and held out to her the gold sceptre that was in his hand. So Esther*
*approached and touched the tip of the sceptre.*

(Esther 5:1–2)

The scene that has just been portrayed is in a sense a picture of the mercy and grace of God towards each one of us, because our sin should have resulted in our judgement.[26] However, because Jesus laid down His life for us we can now experience God's mercy and grace. Not only does this mean that we can have a relationship with our Heavenly Father now, but also that we will spend eternity with Him.[27]

For Esther, the way in which Xerxes responded to her was undoubtedly the breakthrough that she and others had prayed for; it was the answer to their prayers. Did she perhaps later spend time in thanking and praising God for what had happened? Certainly that should be our response whenever we experience a breakthrough of some kind that is clearly the result of our prayers.

The response that Xerxes made to Esther was an indication that she had won his favour. His actions told her that she was not going to be punished for breaking the protocol of the court. When he then asked Esther what her request was and offered her up to half the kingdom, we see the depth and reality of the incredible favour that was upon her life. However, Esther chose to ignore both of his questions and instead asked him to come to dinner with her in her quarters that evening and to bring Haman with him.[28] Esther's invitation shows us that she knew Xerxes very well. She understood that in spite of the offer he had made to give her up to half the kingdom, he was not yet ready to hear her request, hence the invitation to a banquet with her, for both him and Haman.

Such an invitation would have broken the protocol of the palace. It would have been unusual for Esther to eat with Xerxes, but also, and even more significantly, it would have been virtually unheard of to have another man present on such an occasion.

Was the making of the invitation perhaps prompted by the Holy Spirit in the first place? Whilst we cannot clearly say one way or another, the Holy Spirit does get people to do some rather unusual things at times. A good example of this is the Hebridean Revival, which started when some women knocked on a table after being prompted by the Holy Spirit to do so, but there are numerous other examples of this both historically and Biblically.

The two men go with Esther immediately to the women's quarters for the banquet she has prepared for them all. Whilst they are enjoying some wine together, Xerxes again asks Esther what her request is and again offers her up to half of the kingdom.

Once again Esther sidesteps both the question and the offer, preferring to ask the men to dinner again the following night when she says that she will answer Xerxes' question.[29] This suggests that again Esther felt he was not yet ready to hear what she had to say and/or that she was prompted by the Holy Spirit to issue the second invitation. However, once again the Bible does not tell us so we cannot be definitive about it.

It looks as if Esther showed great wisdom in the way she dealt with Xerxes, and that could only have come from God.[30] Wisdom is something we all need, and in James 1:5–7 we read that:

*If any of you lacks wisdom, he should ask God, who gives gen-erously to all without finding fault, and it will be given to him. But when he asks, he must believe and not doubt, because he who doubts is like a wave of the sea, blown and tossed by the wind. That man should not think he will receive anything from the Lord; he is a double-minded man, unstable in all he does.*

Of course the Biblical character most famed for his wisdom was King Solomon. His prayer asking God for wisdom is given in 1 Kings 3:4–15, as is the Lord's response to Solomon, should you want to read about it for yourself. The important thing to know is that because Solomon had asked the Lord for wisdom rather than riches, fame or a long life, God promised him those things as well as giving him what he originally asked for. You may also like to read the story about the baby in 1 Kings 3:16–28 as the way Solomon dealt with that situation shows us clearly that God had answered his prayer for wisdom. It is worth noting that God kept this promise to Solomon. This teaches us that God is truly faithful to His promises and we can therefore be confident that ours will also be fulfilled.

## Endnote References

| | |
|---|---|
| 1 | Nehemiah 1:1–11 |
| 2 | Esther 4:4–5 |
| 3 | 1 Corinthians 12:15 |
| 4 | 1 Corinthians 12:25 |
| 5 | Esther 4:8–9 |
| 6 | Leviticus 23:26–31 |
| 7 | Leviticus 16:1–28 |
| 8 | John 16:13 |
| 9 | 1 Peter 1:18–20 |
| 10 | Genesis 37:12–36 |
| 11 | Genesis 39:13–20a |
| 12 | Genesis 40:1–22 |
| 13 | Genesis 40:23 |
| 14 | Genesis 41:8–13 |
| 15 | Genesis 41:25–47 |
| 16 | Genesis 47:5–12 |
| 17 | Jeremiah 29:11 |
| 18 | 1 Corinthians 12:7–11 |
| 19 | Ephesians 4:11–13 |
| 20 | Esther 4:15–16 |
| 21 | 1 Peter 1:18–19 |
| 22 | Matthew 4:1–4 |
| 23 | Matthew 6:16–17 |
| 24 | Isaiah 58:1–14 |
| 25 | Habakkuk 2:1 |
| 26 | Romans 5:15–21 |
| 27 | Romans 6:23 |
| 28 | Esther 5:3–4 |
| 29 | Esther 5:5–7 |
| 30 | Psalm 111:10 |

# 5

# HAMAN AND MORDECAI

*Haman went out that day happy and in high spirits. But when he saw Mordecai at the king's gate and observed that he neither rose nor showed fear in his presence, he was filled with rage against Mordecai. Nevertheless, Haman restrained himself and went home.*

(Esther 5:9–10a)

Having just enjoyed the banquet with Esther and Xerxes, Haman was in a good mood, but that changed as soon as he saw Mordecai, because he did not show him the respect that he thought he was due. Like honour, respect is a matter of personal choice,[1] rather than something that can, or should, be demanded from us.

It used to be the case that if people saw someone whose way of life demonstrated that they had integrity, and therefore had what was called a 'good character', they would generally respect that person of their own volition. However, the societal changes of the last twenty years or so have undermined the basis of this to some extent and it no longer happens to the degree that it once did, but that still does not give anyone the right to demand respect from someone else. We live in a world now where people seem to think that they are entitled to have certain things, but some of those things are not theirs to demand.

What is even worse is that this sense of entitlement is infecting church life and there is now a real danger that some leaders could, like Haman, be offended if they do not get the respect, or honour, that they believe to be their rightful due. This is not the kind of behaviour that Jesus modelled throughout His earthly life and that we are called, as His disciples, to emulate. In fact, Paul tells us that:

> *Your attitude should be the same as that of Christ Jesus: Who, being in very nature God, did not consider equality with God something to be grasped, but made himself nothing, taking the very nature of a servant, being made in human likeness. And being found in appearance as a man, he humbled himself and became obedient to death – even death on a cross!*

> (Philippians 2:5–8)

From this one passage we can see that one of the things that should mark us out as the people of God is humility, but obviously not to the point where we become doormats! This is, of course, what lies at the other end of the spectrum to the pride and arrogance that we have just been speaking about, but it is just as wrong.

In the quotation at the start of this chapter, we saw that Haman wanted Mordecai to fear him even if he did not respect him. No authority figure should want the people under their care to be afraid of them, because that will not only hinder them from responding properly to them, but also from doing whatever is being asked of them. Perhaps most importantly, this is not conducive to that individual's well-being, which should be high on the list of priorities of anyone given any sort of leadership or authority role, but all too often seems not to be.

My relationship with my father when I was growing up was such that I was still terrified of him in my late thirties, which negatively affected the way that I related to him. In fact, I never felt particularly comfortable, or safe, with my father, which meant I was always very guarded with him and was therefore unable to share my life as fully with him as I would have liked.

Thankfully God did a lot of healing in my relationship with my father in the late 1980s and early 1990s. This meant that by the time of his death in 1997 I had reached the place where I was able to grieve the loss of never being able to have the relationship with him that I had longed for. I am now at the point where the things that my father did that damaged me have receded into the background, whilst the good things that he gave me are now in the foreground whenever I think about him. Whilst working through the various issues involved with God has been a long journey, it has proved to be an extremely worthwhile one as it has brought about a deeper relationship with Him.

We are told that Haman became enraged when Mordecai failed to respond to him, although he did manage to restrain himself until he got home. What we are not told is whether he took his temper out on anyone, or anything. So often, this is what happens when someone has anger issues, as Haman obviously did.

Once he got home, Haman got together with his wife, Zeresh, his family and his friends, so that he could brag to them about his wealth, his sons and the various ways in which King Xerxes had honoured him.[2] It looks as if, having not got what he hoped for from Mordecai, Haman's ego needed bolstering, so he got together a group of people who would tell him how great he was, thus restoring his sense of well-being.

We may have met people like Haman at some point and noticed the way in which others will try to placate them in order to have a quiet life. However, this approach does not deal with the problem and will in fact reinforce that person's behaviour, making them increasingly difficult to deal with. Having said that, as we learned with Vashti, pride comes before a fall, and as we shall see, Haman does in fact come unstuck later in the story.

As Christians we are commanded to love one another,[3] but that is not particularly easy to do when someone – whether they are in authority over us or not – has attitudes, or patterns of behaviour, that make them difficult to cope with. For example, dealing with someone who will not admit that they got things wrong requires a lot of patience and wisdom. I know this from personal experience as that was one of the issues in my relationship with my father! Regarding such relationship challenges we need to remember what it says in Proverbs 27:17:

*As iron sharpens iron, so one man sharpens another.*

In other words, a certain amount of conflict in a relationship will produce growth and maturity in us if we do not allow it to become a stumbling block but use it instead as a building block for our personal development. The primary key to being able to do this lies in our partnership with the Holy Spirit and in seeking Him for wisdom in dealing with the issues in question.

Going back to Haman, we are now told that he goes on to say:

*And that's not all ... I'm the only person Queen Esther invited to accompany the king to the banquet she gave. And she has invited me along with the king tomorrow. But all this gives me no satisfaction as long as I see that Jew Mordecai sitting at the king's gate.*

(Esther 5:12–13)

Having finished bragging, Haman now seemingly asks those around him for their advice about his problem with Mordecai, perhaps knowing that by doing so he is tying the whole group even more tightly to him by making them complicit in what will happen. The way in which Haman phrases his comment about Mordecai is rather manipulative, but then people with the kind of issues we have been discussing generally are, because this is how they ensure that their needs are met and their ego is bolstered.

Zeresh responds by suggesting that Haman should build some gallows and the next morning ask the king to have Mordecai hanged upon them. She then encourages Haman to go and enjoy the banquet with the queen after he has done so – all of which he happily takes on board.[4] By suggesting this kind of action, Zeresh encouraged Haman further down the path of self-destruction and demonstrated a lack of real concern for his well-being.

Most people do not like confrontation, and probably Zeresh was too scared of Haman to challenge him as she should have done about his attitude and behaviour. However, learning how to bring Godly correction to those around us when it is required is part of the journey into Christian maturity.[5] Sadly, it seems that all too many Christians go running to their pastors whenever they have a problem with someone, rather than following the process that Jesus gave us for sorting out our issues with one another.[6] This is not fair on the pastor in question, who should not be expected to deal with problems that could probably be sorted out without their involvement. To put it another way, we should only go to our pastors with the kind of issues that we are not able to deal with ourselves.

Apparently, the king could not sleep that night and for some reason he decided to look at the records of his reign, so he had them brought in and read to him. As a result, Xerxes discovered that Mordecai had never been rewarded for his part in uncovering the conspiracy to assassinate him (we looked at this earlier in the book).[7]

Did God perhaps ensure that King Xerxes learned of this event at this time in order to protect Mordecai? The Bible does not tell us, but there are several Biblical stories where it is obvious that God intervened and rescued people from something,[8] or someone. It is more than probable that He did so in this case too, because of the way in which various circumstances suddenly came together. In fact, I can think of moments in my life where certain events have converged suddenly in such an amazing way that I know that what happened is not just a coincidence. I am sure that most people can think of similar occasions.

Returning to the story:

*The king said, 'Who is in the court?' Now Haman had just entered the outer court of the palace to speak to the king about hanging*

*Mordecai on the gallows he had erected for him. His attendants answered, 'Haman is standing in the court.' 'Bring him in,' the king ordered. When Haman entered, the king asked him, 'What should be done for the man the king delights to honour?' Now Haman thought to himself, 'Who is there that the king would rather honour than me?'*

(Esther 6:4–6)

The fact that Haman assumed that Xerxes was talking about him speaks volumes not only about his pride, but also his arrogance and complacency. His assumption that he was the one being spoken of colours what he says in response to Xerxes' question. As we see below, the answer that he gives is a reflection of his own desires and longings, rather than what someone else might want as their reward:

*For the man the king delights to honour, have them bring a royal robe the king has worn and a horse the king has ridden, one with a royal crest placed on its head. Then let the robe and horse be entrusted to one of the king's most noble princes. Let them robe the man the king delights to honour, and lead him on the horse through the city streets, proclaiming before him, 'This is what is done for the man the king delights to honour!'*

(Esther 6:7–9)

It is obvious that Haman secretly coveted Xerxes' throne; he wanted what he had, hence the nature of the suggestions that he made to the king regarding the reward. Coveting something, as Haman obviously did, is inherently destructive, just as any form of lust is.

When we recognise that a situation of this kind has arisen in our lives, we need to deal with it as quickly as we can, because otherwise we can find ourselves in a place that we may not easily be able to come back from. God hates sin not just because it is wrong, but even more importantly because of the way in which it damages us as individuals, and hurts all those who are affected by it. God warns us about the consequences of committing sin because He is a good Father who loves us and wants us to have the kind of lives that have not been marred by such things. God's heart towards us is summed up rather beautifully in Jeremiah 29:11:

> *'I know the plans I have for you,' declares the LORD, 'plans to prosper you and not to harm you, plans to give you hope and a future.'*

Returning to the story, we now read that Xerxes tells Haman to go and do for Mordecai all that he suggested.[9] The obvious question to ask at this point is: Could God have been the one behind the discovery that Xerxes made about Mordecai? There are many stories of God disturbing, or waking, His people in the night for one reason or another. As we have seen, even though Xerxes was not one of God's people it seems a distinct possibility, since it stopped Haman from being able to take the action that he wanted against Mordecai. Instead of having him hanged, Haman now has no choice but to give him the kind of honour that he himself wanted to be given. As becomes apparent further on in the story, this caused him intense distress. We can see from what is said next that Haman did exactly what he had suggested to Xerxes for Mordecai, down to the last detail. Having done that, he went home and told Zeresh, his family and his friends all that had happened.[10]

The response that Haman got from them is rather telling and quite extraordinary:

*His advisers and his wife Zeresh said to him, 'Since Mordecai, before whom your downfall has started, is of Jewish origin, you cannot stand against him – you will surely come to ruin!' While they were still talking with him, the king's eunuchs arrived and hurried Haman away to the banquet Esther had prepared.*

(Esther 6:13b–14)

Haman's wife and those with them clearly understood something of the nature and character of the God worshipped by the Jews of their time, and also by us today. This is why they talked about Haman's downfall as they did. As we will shortly see, the words that they spoke were prophetic in nature and spoke directly into the consequences of Haman's actions.

At the banquet, once again when they were all drinking wine, Xerxes asked Esther the same questions, as well as making her the same offer as he had the previous day. This time, whilst Esther chose to ignore the offer, she answered the questions.

However, before doing so, she started by pleading for her life and the lives of her people. Xerxes responded by asking her who their adversary was, and when Esther told him it was Haman, he became angry and went out into the garden.[11] There are some obvious questions to ask at this point, starting with: What exactly was it that made Xerxes angry? Was it because he felt that Haman had betrayed the trust that he had put in him, or was it because of the impact of Haman's actions on Esther? Since we are not told we cannot be certain, but it seems possible that the answer to the first question lies in answering 'yes' to both the second and third questions.

When someone we trust betrays us in some way it can be devastating – and the closer that person is to us, the greater the damage will be. The way in which Jesus was betrayed with a kiss creates a picture for us of what the betrayal of a friend can look and feel like.[12] However, unlike Jesus we will not necessarily see it coming,[13] which is why Proverbs 4:23 says:

*Above all else, guard your heart, for it is the wellspring of life.*

Doing so, however, does not mean putting up a lot of barriers around ourselves, because that will negatively impact how close we can get to those with whom we want an intimate relationship, including God. The best way to guard our hearts involves giving our heart to God and asking Him to watch over it. Whilst this will not stop people from being able to hurt us, it will stop us from being as badly hurt as we would otherwise have been.

Learning how to guard our heart is particularly important when it comes to those we care about the most. This is because seeing someone that we love being hurt by a person we trusted is one of the hardest things we will ever have to deal with in life. What makes it even harder is when the suffering of the one we love goes on and on, seemingly without end, as that person may then begin to feel our pain, which will in turn magnify theirs. Thankfully, although the situation may seem impossible to us, nothing is impossible for God[14] and, if we hand the situation over to Him completely instead of trying to find our own way of dealing with it, He can and will intervene in some way, although it may not be quite in the way that we are expecting.

Going back to the story, we read that:

*Just as the king returned from the palace garden to the banquet hall, Haman was falling on the couch where Esther was reclining. The king exclaimed, 'Will he even molest the queen while she is with me in the house?'*

(Esther 7:8a)

Based on what he had heard just a few minutes earlier, Xerxes made a judgement without finding out the facts first, something most of us have done at some point in our lives. It is all too easy to stick labels on people; we have probably all done it, but it can lead to people being ill-treated, particularly if that label is very emotive in nature. It is for this reason that Jesus told us not to judge others.[15] What we need to do instead is to ask the Holy Spirit to enable us to see people as He sees them. We will then be able to see their areas of weakness and difficulty through the lens of love, which should lead to us relating and dealing with them in the way that Jesus wants us to.

Continuing with the scene in the palace:

*As soon as the word left the king's mouth, they covered Haman's face. Then Harbona, one of the eunuchs attending the king, said, 'A gallows seventy-five feet high stands by Haman's house. He had it made for Mordecai, who spoke up to help the king.'*

(Esther 7:8b–9b)

Obviously, the purpose of the gallows that Haman had built was common knowledge in the palace, so that begs the question: How did that come about? Was it the result of palace gossip?

That seems very likely, but who was the source of it? Zeresh or another member of Haman's family? One of Haman's supposed friends? Since we are not told how Harbona came to know about the gallows, we cannot be certain who told him, but it is obvious from the way in which he disclosed the information that he was not happy with Haman's reason for having it built in the first place.

Gossip can be very destructive, damaging lives and reputations,[16] which is why we should not take part in it. I have seen the impact of gossip on many people's lives over the years and am personally aware of a situation where it was the primary cause of someone attempting to kill themselves.

Haman was of course hanged on the gallows that he intended for Mordecai, which has a certain macabre irony. It speaks to me of 'the law of sowing and reaping', as described in Galatians 6:8:

*The one who sows to please his sinful nature from that nature will reap destruction; the one who sows to please the Spirit, from the Spirit will reap eternal life.*

It is relatively easy for us to see this principle at work in Haman's life, but what about our own? What kind of life are we living? Are we living to please God? Earlier on in the same epistle we read:

*live by the Spirit, and you will not gratify the desires of the sinful nature. For the sinful nature desires what is contrary to the Spirit, and the Spirit what is contrary to the sinful nature. They are in conflict with each other, so that you do not do what you want. But if you are led by the Spirit, you are not under law.*

(Galatians 5:16–18)

These verses teach us that the key to discovering God's heart for us is living in the Spirit. That is what will enable us to live the kind of holy life that will please God.

## ENDNOTE REFERENCES

| | |
|---|---|
| 1 | 1 PETER 2:17 |
| 2 | ESTHER 5:10B–11 |
| 3 | 1 JOHN 4:19–21 |
| 4 | ESTHER 5:14 |
| 5 | GALATIANS 6:1 |
| 6 | MATTHEW 18:15–17 |
| 7 | ESTHER 6:1–3 |
| 8 | DANIEL 6:6–27 |
| 9 | ESTHER 6:10 |
| 10 | ESTHER 5:11–13A |
| 11 | ESTHER 7:1–7A |
| 12 | MATTHEW 26:47–50 |
| 13 | MATTHEW 26:20–25 |
| 14 | LUKE 1:37 |
| 15 | LUKE 6:36–37 |
| 16 | PROVERBS 26:20 |

# 6

# ESTHER AND THE SECOND EDICT

*That same day King Xerxes gave Queen Esther the estate of Haman, the enemy of the Jews. And Mordecai came into the presence of the king, for Esther had told how he was related to her. The king took off his signet ring, which he had reclaimed from Haman, and presented it to Mordecai. And Esther appointed him over Haman's estate.*

(Esther 8:1–2)

Xerxes did not have to give Esther Haman's estate; the fact that he did so points to the possibility that he loved her. Such a generous gift is not something that a person would give to someone they did not have feelings for. This gift can be seen as a picture of the mercy and grace of God in saving us,[1] because just as Esther had done little to deserve being given the estate, so the same is true for us with regard to the gift of salvation. Paul speaks about this in Ephesians 2:8–9:

*For it is by grace you have been saved, through faith – and this not from yourselves, it is the gift of God – not by works, so that no-one can boast.*

Since Esther had revealed her identity, she no longer had to conceal her relationship to Mordecai, all of which must have been incredibly liberating for her. It must also have been such an incredible joy for her to be able to give something back to her adopted father and mentor, Mordecai, for all that he had done for her over the years.

King Xerxes promoted Mordecai to the position that Haman had previously occupied, whilst Esther gave him the stewardship of what had once been Haman's estate. These two linked promotions are in a sense a picture of the work of restoration that God wants to do in the life of every one of His children.[2] The story of Job paints a picture of this core Kingdom principle[3] and has much to teach us about what that restoration could look like for us.

When we have been hurt badly by others, we start to subconsciously create all sorts of mechanisms to protect ourselves. Such masks also obscure our identity, which means that how we present ourselves to others is no longer a true reflection of the person we are inside. This starts to change as we progressively seek God's heart for us by partnering with the Holy Spirit. He starts healing our wounds as part of the restoration process that happens in our lives as we press into God's heart for us. This process, often referred to as 'sanctification', also brings about the transformation[4] that will result in the incarnating of the character of Christ in our lives.[5] Moreover, we will increasingly experience the freedom that comes as a result, and the joy it gives.

We now read that:

*Esther again pleaded with the king, falling at his feet and weeping. She begged him to put to an end to the evil plan of Haman the Agagite, which he had devised against the Jews. Then the king extended the gold sceptre to Esther and she arose and stood before him.*                                          (Esther 8:3–4)

In this quotation we can see a beautiful picture of intercession, which generally starts with us humbling ourselves before God[6] and often involves grief and/or repentance. The golden sceptre here is thus a picture of God's mercy and grace being extended towards us in such times, drawing us into a dialogue with Him.[7]

Having humbled herself before Xerxes, and been given the opportunity to speak freely, Esther now puts in her request for him to overrule the decree that Haman had made previously on behalf of the king.[8] Esther also spoke of her personal distress at the implications of that edict,[9] and here we see the way in which true intercession involves more than just words.

True intercession flows out of our hearts, the core of who we are, and as such engages not just our minds but also our hearts and spirits. It is also without a doubt the most rewarding, but also the most sacrificial, type of prayer spoken of in the Bible. As such, whilst God may call any one of us into a season of intercession, not all of us are intercessors – individuals who can disappear into their prayer room for weeks, months and even, in some cases, years!

Moving on to the king's response to Esther:

*King Xerxes replied to Queen Esther and to Mordecai the Jew,*

*'Because Haman attacked the Jews, I have given his estate to Esther, and they have hanged him on the gallows. Now write another decree in the king's name on behalf of the Jews as seems best to you, and seal it with the king's signet ring – for no document written in the king's name and sealed with his ring can be revoked.'*

(Esther 8:7–8)

From this we can see that the favour of God was all over the situation, because Xerxes agreed immediately to Esther's request. We also learn that the previous edict could not be revoked because there was no mechanism for doing so.[10] This meant that in order to counter it another one would have to be written. Esther's intercession with Xerxes opened his heart and gave Mordecai the authority to make the necessary decree.

We have just been talking about a 'natural' decree, but decrees can also be made that are spiritual in nature.[11] Such decrees are based on Kingdom principles and are made in partnership with the Holy Spirit. They are therefore prophetic in character and are endued with creative power.[12] This is part of the 'governmental' role of the Church and is a vital part of advancing the Kingdom of God – the reign and rule of Christ – spoken of in Matthew 28:16–20. That passage is in fact an important key in understanding what our call to discipleship is about and describes another aspect of the main aim of the Christian life. This, at its simplest, is not just becoming like Christ, but also doing the greater things that He promised we would do.[13]

The process of writing the new edict and how it was dispatched is described in detail in Esther 8:9–10. However, since it is the same as the earlier one,[14] we will move straight on to what was said in it:

*The king's edict granted the Jews in every city the right to assemble and protect themselves; to destroy, kill and annihilate any armed force of any nationality or province that might attack them and their women and children; and to plunder the property of their enemies.*

(Esther 8:11)

From our perspective this may seem rather harsh, but if we look at it in terms of the time and the culture – as well as of course the context of the story – it begins to become much more understandable. Because the laws of Persia could not be repealed,[15] this edict was the only way to reverse the impact of the one that had been made by Haman.

To put it another way, this was without a doubt the only way for the Jewish people to be saved from destruction. In that sense, it was probably the outworking of God's justice for them. We too can experience situations where, because of their very nature, the only way for them to be turned around is far from ideal. It is therefore of vital importance that if we see something going on in someone's life that does not appear to be right, we do not just rush in, all guns blazing, but spend time in seeking the Lord and asking Him what He wants us to do about it – if anything.

In God's economy timing is everything,[16] and this was certainly the case with the date that was set for the Jews to enact the new decree:

*The day appointed for the Jews to do this in all the provinces of King Xerxes was the thirteenth day of the twelfth month, the month of Adar.*
(Esther 8:12)

If we think back to the date given in Haman's decree, we can see it is the same day and month. In other words, Mordecai's decree came into force on the same day Haman's did and would therefore nullify the impact of it. Most of us will have had the experience of situations that worked out far better than should have been the case, after we have cried out to God. As we shall see later in the book, this second decree turned things around for the Jews in all sorts of unexpected ways.

Our God is truly the God of the impossible,[17] and the Bible is full of stories that teach us this. Let us look at just one of them, a story from the life of Elisha. This story begins with a widow coming to him because she is in debt, and the person to whom she owes the money is threatening to take her sons to be his slaves. Elisha's heart is moved, so he starts by asking her what he can do. He then follows that up by asking what she has in the house.[18] After she tells him that she has some oil, Elisha says to her:

*Go round and ask all your neighbours for empty jars. Don't ask for just a few. Then go inside and shut the door behind you and your sons. Pour oil into all the jars, and as each is filled, put it to one side.*

(2 Kings 4:3–4)

Such advice would probably sound ridiculous to many people, particularly those who do not understand the way things work in God's Kingdom, which is an upside-down kingdom[19] where things do not necessarily go the way we might expect. Whilst at times God will break into our lives in a dramatic way, He will generally work through our circumstances (although He is not of course limited by them) to bring about the breakthrough that we are seeking from Him. It is for this reason that we need to learn to listen to His promptings and be able to recognise His voice clearly. This is what the woman in this story did. Her obedience led to a miracle that radically changed her situation and that of her sons.[20]

The story of this woman involved some of the same ingredients that we saw in the deliverance of the Jews through Esther. In other words, by looking at the two stories side by side we can learn something of the principles required for us to see a breakthrough of some kind in our lives. Let us sum up the three core principles involved:

1.  Both Esther and the woman in the Elisha story found themselves in impossible situations: they were desperate.

2.  Both women sought help from God; they looked to Him in faith for a breakthrough.

3.  Both women did what they were told to do; they were obedient, and their obedience brought the blessing that they sought.

Desperation, faith and obedience will bring about a breakthrough in our lives, particularly if we do not make the mistake of telling God what to do or how to do it, but instead leave the outcome in His hands!

It is so important to be obedient to God. That is the measure of our love for Him, as can be seen from the following scripture:

*This is love for God: to obey his commands. And his commands are not burdensome, for everyone born of God overcomes the world. This is the victory that has overcome the world, even our faith.*

*Who is it that overcomes the world? Only he who believes that Jesus is the Son of God.*

(1 John 5:3–5)

These verses not only link love for God with obedience, but also clearly indicate that that is what will enable us to overcome 'the world', which represents the temptations that we face every day to do what we want rather than what God wants.

Going back to the Persian edict, copies of it were sent out across the empire by couriers in much the same way as the previous one.[21] Whilst today we can communicate with people on the other side of the world by phone or through the internet, it must have taken weeks for these messengers, travelling on horseback, to reach the four corners of the empire. We need to recognise facts like these if we are to understand the background of this and other Biblical stories.

To put it another way, when we are looking at the Bible it is of vital importance to recognise the social and cultural differences between that time and ours as that plays into our understanding of what Scripture is saying. This in turn can affect our understanding of the principles of our journey into God's heart for us.

The day when Mordecai was promoted and the decree was sent out must have been rather a bittersweet day for him. Nevertheless:

*Mordecai left the king's presence wearing royal garments of blue and white, a large crown of gold and a purple robe of fine linen. And the city of Susa held a joyous celebration. For the Jews it was a time of happiness and joy, gladness and honour.*

(Esther 8:15b–16)

What we see in these verses was certainly not an outcome that Mordecai had looked for, or even expected. However, it seems probable that when Haman had led him around the streets of Susa on one of the king's horses[22] this may have been a prophetic act that led to it being birthed.

The Bible is full of such prophetic acts. For example, the men of a certain city came to Elijah because the water from one of their wells was bad and the land around it was not productive. Elijah got them to bring him a new bowl with some salt in it. He then tipped the salt into the well, and not only was it healed, but the land around it was too.[23]

Stories such as this show us that God's ways are not ours and that what we think or expect Him to do may not be the way He will choose to do things. For another example, we need only to look at the circumstances surrounding the birth of Jesus. None of us would have expected the Son of God to be born as a baby to an unmarried woman of seemingly little account[24] in a cattle shed in a town that was something of a backwater, and yet He was.[25]

In one of his letters Paul tells us that:

*God chose the foolish things of the world to shame the wise; God chose the weak things of the world to shame the strong. He chose the lowly things of this world and the despised things – and the things that are not – to nullify the things that are, so that no-one may boast before him.*

(1 Corinthians 1:27–29)

Reading the Bible teaches us that God likes to call the most unlikely people into places and situations of significance in His purposes. Just looking at the stories of Gideon, Ruth, David and Peter shows us the truth of this. Beyond the Bible, looking at those around us, and perhaps even ourselves, we can see this principle at work.

Moreover, just as Mordecai was reclothed by His king, so the same is true for each one of us. When we surrender our lives to Jesus, we are justified through our faith in Him[26] and are clothed in His righteousness.[27] However, it is important for us all to remember that justification and sanctification are two different, but interconnected, aspects of holiness and that both are essential elements of our journey into God's heart for us. Holiness – and humility – are aspects of the character of Jesus, along with the fruit of the Spirit,[28] and this is what will be incarnated into our lives as we partner with Him.

Whilst we might not be fully in accord with the reasons for the joyful celebration that was held by the Jews in the city of Susa, we need to be aware of the level of oppression that they had suffered for generations and how this would have affected them. It was obviously not just about celebrating Mordecai's promotion or the chance for them to get revenge on their enemies, but also, and more importantly, it was about the incredible way in which their prayers had been answered. What they were celebrating most of all is that God had heard their cries and had intervened on their behalf, so they now knew without a shadow of a doubt that He had not forgotten them or, for that matter, His promises to them.

We now read that:

*In every province and in every city, wherever the edict of the king*
*went, there was joy and gladness among the Jews, with feasting*

*and celebrating. And many people of other nationalities became Jews because fear of the Jews had seized them.*

(Esther 8:17)

The last part of this verse speaks volumes about the impact of this edict on the lives of the people of the Persian empire. For people to want to become Jews indicates that their fear of being considered an enemy of the Jews was far greater than that of being persecuted for being one! This begs all sorts of questions, from what proportion of the population was Jewish to how many of those who became Jews thought they might escape justice by doing so. Since the Bible does not give us the answer to such questions, we are not able to address them, but being aware of the issues involved does give us insight into what was going on.

Perhaps here we need to recognise that having unanswered questions about things in the Bible, or about other things, can either be a stepping-stone or a stumbling block to us in our life of faith. If we choose to give our questions to God and trust Him to tell us what we need to know at the right time, then they will become building blocks in our life with Him, but if we choose not to, we may find that we lose our way and are shipwrecked as a result.

One of the things we can learn from this part of the Esther story is the need to celebrate the good things that God does in our lives – and in the lives of those around us. Testimonies can be a wonderful way of doing this. We can learn so much about God's heart for us as individuals from each other's stories. However, it is not often that people are given the opportunity to share publicly the wonderful things that God has been, or is, doing in their lives. This is a pity as I have been in meetings where someone has shared a healing testimony and that healing has been multiplied into the lives of some of those listening.

Sharing our stories about what God has done for us will have another kind of impact in our lives too, as is made plain in Revelation 12:10–11:

> *Then I heard a loud voice in heaven say: 'Now have come the salvation and the power and the kingdom of our God, and the authority of his Christ. For the accuser of our brothers, who accuses them before our God day and night, has been hurled down. They overcame him by the blood of the Lamb and by the word of their testimony; they did not love their lives so much as to shrink from death.'*

Sharing what God has done in our lives will enable us to overcome the enemy's lies and works, enabling us to take ground in Kingdom terms. This is part of the process involved for each one of us in seeing the fulfilment of God's promises to us as individuals.

# ENDNOTE REFERENCES

1       JOHN 3:16–18
2       JOEL 2:25–26
3       JOB 42:12–13
4       2 CORINTHIANS 3:18
5       GALATIANS 5:22–23
6       2 CHRONICLES 7:14
7       GENESIS 18:16–32
8       ESTHER 8:5
9       ESTHER 8:6
10      DANIEL 6:15
11      JEREMIAH 51:12
12      2 KINGS 8:1
13      JOHN 14:12
14      ESTHER 3:12–14
15      DANIEL 6:8
16      ECCLESIASTES 3:1–8
17      LUKE 1:37
18      2 KINGS 4:1–2
19      ISAIAH 55:8–9
20      2 KINGS 4:5–7
21      ESTHER 8:13–14
22      ESTHER 6:11
23      2 KINGS 2:19–22
24      MATTHEW 1:18–23
25      LUKE 2:15–18
26      ROMANS 5:1–2
27      ROMANS 9:30-31; GALATIANS 3:26–27
28      GALATIANS 5:22–24

# 7

# JUSTICE AT LAST?

*On the thirteenth day of the twelfth month, the month of Adar, the edict commanded by the king was to be carried out. On this day the enemies of the Jews had hoped to overpower them, but now the tables were turned and the Jews got the upper hand over those who hated them.*

(Esther 9:1)

As we saw in the previous chapter, allowing the second decree and all that would happen as a result of it was the only way that God could give the Jews justice in what was an impossible situation. Otherwise He would have had to intervene supernaturally, and as has been said, this is not generally the way God operates in our lives. The Bible gives us a progressive revelation of the character and nature of God, which is one of the reasons we need to read it. Justice is one of the aspects of His character that Scripture speaks of. Looking at just one verse, Psalm 89:14, we read:

*Righteousness and justice are the foundation of your throne; love
and faithfulness go before you.*

This one verse alone speaks not only about God's justice but
also His righteousness, love and faithfulness, so immediately
we can see four aspects of His character and nature. Reading
the Bible will teach us, for example, that:

- God is the King of Kings and Lord of Lords (God is
  sovereign);
- He is all-powerful (He is omnipotent);
- He is ever present (He is omnipresent);
- He is all-knowing (He is omniscient);
- He is merciful;
- He is gracious;
- He is compassionate;
- He is holy;
- He is eternal;
- He is immutable (He is unchanging);
- He is the one who will judge us all at the end of time.[1]

These characteristics are all enfolded and held together by His
unconditional love, today described as the 'Father heart' of
God. Together they give us an idea of what a balanced picture
of His character and nature should look like. Once we begin to
understand that, we can then build a more intimate relationship with God, because true intimacy is built on an increasing
and deepening understanding of the other person involved in
the relationship.

Returning to the story of Esther, we read that:

*The Jews assembled in their cities in all the provinces of King Xerxes to attack those seeking their destruction. No-one could stand against them, because the people of all the other nationalities were afraid of them.*

(Esther 9:2)

How do we view a situation such as this, considering what we believe about who God is, and the fact that one of the Ten Commandments prohibits murder?[2] Such questions are not easily answered, and theologians have grappled with issues such as these for thousands of years. The simplest way to see this type of situation is in the light of God's 'permissive will'; in other words it is something that God has allowed to happen. This does not mean that it is in accord with God's perfect will, but that knowing the various factors involved, He has chosen to allow it. Nor does it mean that there will not be consequences for those involved further down the road.

Continuing from the previous verse:

*And all the nobles of the provinces, the satraps, the governors and the king's administrators helped the Jews, because fear of Mordecai had seized them. Mordecai was prominent in the palace; his reputation spread throughout the provinces, and he became more and more powerful.*

(Esther 9:3–4)

What an amazing breakthrough for the Jewish people and for Mordecai! Such breakthroughs can seem to happen very speedily, but we have no idea how long Mordecai waited for things to change for his people,[3] or for that matter how many hours he and other Jews spent in intercession before things finally changed for their people.

The story goes on:

*The Jews struck down all their enemies with the sword, killing and destroying them, and they did what they pleased to those who hated them.*

(Esther 9:5)

Whilst we may find the way in which the Jews slaughtered their enemies deeply distressing or hard to stomach, we need to recognise that Esther does not tell us about the persecution they had endured, or what they suffered as a result. It is all too easy to look at people and situations without understanding the story behind what we are seeing, and sit in judgement, but that is not the way God wants us to live. We are told that God looks at the heart,[4] and that is what we need to do in partnership with the Holy Spirit, starting of course with our own heart.[5]

There is a story from the life of Jesus in which He is questioned about 'the traditions of men'.[6] Here He speaks about the heart, which Biblically refers to the core of who we are rather than the organ that pumps blood around our bodies. The quotation that follows gives us the crux of what Jesus has to say on the subject:

*the things that come out of the mouth come from the heart, and these make a man 'unclean'. For out of the heart come evil thoughts, murder, adultery, sexual immorality, theft, false testimony, slander. These are what make a man 'unclean'; but eating with unwashed hands does not make him 'unclean'.* (Matthew 15:18–20)

Verses such as these can hit us hard, and those who are at all self-righteous may find themselves wanting to justify themselves! However, sometimes God has to offend our mind to get to our heart. This is the part of us that He most wants to reach as it is the part of us that most needs to change.

As can be seen from Psalm 51:1–17, David clearly understood the importance of the heart in terms of his relationship with God, and there is therefore a lot that we can learn from his life. Whilst, like all of us, David was not perfect, as can be seen from this psalm he had the humility to admit his mistakes and to put them right with God. Putting things right with God is a vital part of our journey into His heart for us.[7] It is likely that God may then ask us to put things right with those we have hurt[8] and perhaps even to make restitution of some kind to them as the outworking of our repentance.

Back in the late 1980s, I was convicted by the Holy Spirit of the need to ask God to forgive me for my attitude and behaviour towards a certain group of individuals. Having put things right with God, I then became aware of the need to put things right with the people in question. Therefore, I began to approach them individually. If I could speak to someone in person I did so, but if I was not able to, I wrote to them. Most of the people involved were receptive and positive, but some were, to put it mildly, not at all open to my putting things right with them – so I learned that doing what God asks in this kind of situation is not always welcomed! I realised a while afterwards that in all probability my attempt to put things right had been too long in the coming for some people. Since that time, I have tried to ensure that I go to people sooner rather than later.

Going back to the Esther story, we are now told that the Jews killed five hundred men in Susa, as well as killing Haman's ten sons, but did not seize any of the property of these people.[9] On hearing of this, King Xerxes said to Esther:

*The Jews have killed and destroyed five hundred men and the ten sons of Haman in the citadel of Susa. What have they done in the rest of the king's provinces? Now what is your petition? It will be given you. What is your request? It will also be granted.*

(Esther 9:12)

The words spoken by Xerxes reveal the high regard that he had for Esther, as well as showing us again the favour God had given Esther. Her response was to ask Xerxes for another day for citizens of Susa to avenge themselves on their enemies and for Haman's sons to be hanged publicly.[10] Having agreed to do these things, Xerxes had another edict issued in Susa so that the Jews could do as Esther had requested.

The next day the Jews in Susa killed three hundred more of their enemies and Haman's sons were hanged on gallows for all to see. Again, they did not seize any of their enemies' plunder.[11] For some of us at least, these events are rather horrific, especially with regard to what was done to Haman's sons, but we must not let that blind us to the spiritual treasure hidden in the book of Esther which has so much to teach us about God and His heart for us.

The story then switches from what is happening in Susa as a result of the second edict to what had happened in the provinces. We are told that the Jews there killed seventy-five thousand of their enemies but once again did not seize any of their property.[12] This clearly indicates that all they wanted was an end to the persecution they had been experiencing and that they did not do what they did for either financial or material gain.

Most of us have gone, or will go, through periods where things are unusually tough. During such seasons we can become extremely desperate for our lives to change, but it can sometimes be a rather long time before that happens. I can remember one such season back in the 1990s where the following scripture just kept on coming up:

> *Consider it pure joy . . . whenever you face trials of many kinds, because you know that the testing of your faith develops perseverance. Perseverance must finish its work so that you may be mature and complete, not lacking anything.*

> (James 1:2–4)

When it came up for the fourth or fifth time in less than two days, I ended up in stitches; I could not stop laughing for what seemed to be hours but was in fact just a few minutes! I then knew that God was speaking to me about what I was going through, and my heart attitude to what was happening at that time shifted considerably. This obviously made the situation that I was in far less stressful and therefore easier to navigate to its conclusion.

When we go through difficult seasons, we can choose to allow them to make us miserable or we can choose to use them in a more positive way to press into God. To put it another way, the difficulties that we go through can be stumbling blocks, taking us off the road that will lead us into our land of promise, or building blocks that will enable us to enter into all that God has for us.

The fact that the Jews chose not to seize the plunder of those who had been persecuting them is something to be admired, particularly in the light of the 'compensation culture' of today. Obviously, it is not wrong to seek compensation in certain circumstances, but things are now going too far and people seek compensation for what are relatively minor situations. As Christians we need to prayerfully consider when, or even whether, we should pursue such action after we have worked through the circumstances that might warrant it.

Again, for some of us, the idea that the day after killing their enemies, which was the fourteenth of Adar in the provinces and the fifteenth in Susa, was for the Jews a day of celebration, involving not just feasting but also the giving of gifts,[13] might also be rather difficult to understand or even to relate to. However, the end of a difficult season can give us such a feeling of release that we want to celebrate. A simple example that most of us can relate to is finishing a course and taking the necessary exams, because there is such a sense of relief when you have completed the last one that you do want to celebrate!

Going back to the story, we read that:

> *Mordecai recorded these events, and he sent letters to all the Jews throughout the provinces of King Xerxes, near and far, to have them celebrate annually the fourteenth and fifteenth days of the month of Adar as the time when the Jews got relief from their enemies, and as the month when their sorrow was turned into joy and their mourning into a day of celebration.*
>
> (Esther 9:20–22a)

The significance of what had happened is shown clearly in Mordecai's instructions about celebrating it on an annual basis. There is a connection between these events and Passover, as both are to do with gaining freedom from something. Both celebrations speak in the same way of the One who is the ultimate deliverer, namely Jesus.[14] In fact all the feasts of the Old Testament speak prophetically about Jesus, although not in quite the same way: some of them tell of His first coming and some of His second.[15] The Feast of Tabernacles, for example, was instituted as a reminder of the way in which the Israelites lived in booths when they left Egypt[16] and speaks of how God was with them throughout their journey into their promised land. This feast speaks prophetically of God living with us and was therefore partially fulfilled in Jesus' first coming but will be completely fulfilled in His second.

Continuing with Mordecai's instructions to the Jews:

*He wrote to them to observe the days as days of feasting and joy and giving presents of food to one another and gifts to the poor. So the Jews agreed to continue the celebration they had begun, doing what Mordecai had written to them.*

(Esther 9:22b–23)

What is particularly noteworthy about Mordecai's letter is the way in which he tells the Jews that the giving of gifts was to be part of the celebration of what is known today as the Feast of Purim.[17] This speaks of the way in which God had blessed them and how, because He had done so, they knew they needed to give something that demonstrated to others their gratitude for that blessing, especially to those less fortunate than themselves.

This is a clear picture for us of the following spiritual principle that Jesus spoke about:

*Give, and it will be given to you. A good measure, pressed down, shaken together and running over, will be poured into your lap. For with the measure you use, it will be measured to you.*

(Luke 6:38)

The previous verse in Luke's Gospel speaks of not judging one another and of the need to forgive,[18] but whilst Jesus connects the principle to judging and forgiveness, it obviously has a wider application. There have been a number of people who, in their books or their preaching, have connected it to the issue of money, but that is not what Jesus is in fact talking about. A careful study of related verses shows us that it is about being generous of heart in the way we live our lives – much more than a superficial reading might indicate.

Another way of looking at this principle is to recognise that God has been more than generous towards us and that since He wants us to be more like Him this means being generous towards those around us. This of course can impact not just the areas that have already been mentioned, but also things like giving your time, and being there for people in whatever way their circumstances require in their hour of need. Having said that, we do need to be careful not to run ourselves ragged trying to meet every need that we see; otherwise we will burn ourselves out. Just because we see a need does not necessarily mean that we should meet it; we need to start by taking the situation to God and asking Him about it – unless the situation is such that it demands instant action from us. For example, if we are at the scene of an accident, or a crime, then we need to act in a way that is appropriate to the situation, as these are things that we cannot just walk away from.

Another good example of this kind of situation is given in the parable of the good Samaritan. This was a story that Jesus told as part of His response to a question from an expert in the Jewish law about what he needed to do in order to inherit eternal life. Jesus starts by asking this expert what it said in the law. The man replies to this by speaking of two commandments; the first was about loving God with every fibre of our being, and the second about loving our neighbour as we love ourselves. Jesus told Him that his answer was a good one, but the expert, having something to prove, then asks Him who his neighbour is.[19]

Jesus starts His reply by saying:

*A man was going down from Jerusalem to Jericho, when he fell into the hands of robbers. They stripped him of his clothes, beat him and went away, leaving him half-dead. A priest happened to be going down the same road, and when he saw the man, he passed by on the other side.* (Luke 10:30–31)

The point that Jesus wants those listening to understand is that the well-being of an individual in dire need is of greater importance to Him than any religious considerations. The priest's primary concern, when faced with a situation involving a man who might perhaps be dead, was his own ceremonial purity – because if he touched a dead body he would then be ceremonially unclean.[20] He chose not to see if he could help the man rather than risk his ceremonial purity.

Jesus then speaks of a Levite who does the same thing for undoubtedly the same reasons,[21] before speaking about the way in which a Samaritan responded to the situation. Those listening to the parable would not have expected the third man not to be a Jew, and the fact that it was a Samaritan would have shocked them to the core. This is because of how Samaritans were seen at this time by the Jews; they would not associate with them for all sorts of historical reasons.

Furthermore, the Samaritan did far more for the man than might have been expected by those listening to the story. He not only tended to his wounds but also took him to the next city where he put him up in an inn. He then continued to look after the man until he needed to leave, but even then, his kindness did not stop. When he left, he told the innkeeper that he would pay for the man's care and that he would do so on his return.[22]

After telling the parable, Jesus asked the expert a question:

*'Which of these three do you think was a neighbour to the man who fell into the hands of robbers?' The expert in the law replied, 'The one who had mercy on him.' Jesus told him, 'Go and do likewise.'*

(Luke 10:36–37)

Mercy, kindness and of course generosity are all aspects of God's character and as such are qualities we should seek to demonstrate in our own lives. More than that, we should be willing to go above and beyond what might be expected in some of the situations that come across our path, because that is what Jesus did in purchasing our salvation. Of course, sometimes our circumstances may be such that we do not have the resources that are required to meet the need in question. However, even in those situations we can at least pray and perhaps even point the needy person towards someone else, or an organisation, that may be able to help them. Certainly, we should not make an excuse like the two men in the parable and walk away without doing anything.

Returning to the book of Esther, we read that:

> *Because of everything written in this letter and because of what they had seen and what had happened to them, the Jews took it upon themselves to establish the custom that they and their descendants and all who join them should without fail observe these two days every year, in the way prescribed and at the time appointed.*

(Esther 9:26b–27)

We are then told that what Mordecai put in his letter Esther confirmed in another, and that she even passed a decree establishing the date and regulations of the Feast of Purim.[23] This feast, along with various others, is still celebrated by the Jews of today.

## ENDNOTE REFERENCES

| | |
|---|---|
| 1 | 1 Corinthians 3:10–15 |
| 2 | Deuteronomy 5:17 |
| 3 | Hebrews 6:12 |
| 4 | 1 Chronicles 28:9 |
| 5 | Matthew 7:1–5 |
| 6 | Matthew 15:1–20 |
| 7 | 1 John 1:8–10 |
| 8 | Matthew 5:23–24 |
| 9 | Esther 9:6–11 |
| 10 | Esther 9:13 |
| 11 | Esther 9:14–15 |
| 12 | Esther 9:16 |
| 13 | Esther 9:17–19 |
| 14 | Luke 4:14–21 |
| 15 | Matthew 24:30–31 |
| 16 | Leviticus 23:33–43 |
| 17 | Esther 9:24–26a |
| 18 | Luke 6:37 |
| 19 | Luke 10:25–29 |
| 20 | Leviticus 21:1–4 |
| 21 | Luke 10:32 |
| 22 | Luke 10:33–35 |
| 23 | Esther 9:28–32 |

# 8

# MORDECAI, ESTHER, JESUS AND US

*King Xerxes imposed tribute throughout the empire, to its distant shores. And all his acts of power and might, together with a full account of the greatness of Mordecai to which the king had raised him, are they not written in the book of the annals of the kings of Media and Persia?*

(Esther 10:1–2)

Did King Xerxes raise Mordecai up to his high position – or did God? This is not an easy question to answer, but it is an important one for us all to consider. We need to recognise that whether God did or not, He certainly could have done, because He has the ability to do so. More than that, if God did not want Mordecai to be promoted in the way that he was, He could have easily prevented it, so let us assume that He did make it all happen. Grasping this point is vital so that we can understand the story of Esther and its significance to us, and also recognise what God is doing in our lives and the lives of those around us.

If our picture of God is too small then our faith to believe what He is able to do in our lives will be restricted too, but if that is not the case, then we will have the faith to believe that God can do the impossible in our lives. Reading the Bible regularly and spending time with God are essential elements in enabling us to build up a true picture of God. This in turn will enable us to have the faith to pray into being the breakthroughs that we are longing to see.

We now come to the last verse of the book of Esther:

*Mordecai the Jew was second in rank to King Xerxes, pre-eminent among the Jews, and held in high esteem by his many fellow Jews, because he worked for the good of his people and spoke up for the welfare of all the Jews.*

(Esther 10:3)

One of the things that the Bible teaches us is that God likes to take nobodies and makes them into somebody. Mordecai is a good example of this, but there are many more such cases in the history of God's people: both Gideon and Ruth are prime examples of this.

Not only that; God likes to take people who are not regarded as having much to offer, or who have been written off by society,[1] and use them in all sorts of remarkable ways for His glory. This once again is countercultural as our society has quite set ideas of what success looks like, and what kind of people are going to be successful. As Christians we need to recognise that such beliefs are ungodly and refuse to buy into them. This is because in God's economy obedience is the primary hallmark of success – something Mordecai modelled for us in the way he lived his life.

Moreover, when we read that Mordecai worked for the good of his people, this indicates that he was most probably a good leader, because this is one of the qualities that the Bible speaks of when describing those who are called to shepherd God's people.[2] In New Testament terms a shepherd is generally known as a pastor or an elder.[3] Let us start by looking at what Jesus said in John 10:11 since He is our ultimate model of a good leader:

*I am the good shepherd. The good shepherd lays down his life for the sheep.*

The Bible teaches us that Jesus laid his life down not just metaphorically, but also literally. To look at it another way, Jesus modelled for us a different way of living,[4] one that is in many ways the polar opposite to how people who do not know Him live, as it involves living sacrificially.

Whilst we may not have to lay our lives down physically as He did, it is important for us to remember what Jesus said to all those who wanted to follow Him:

*If anyone would come after me, he must deny himself and take up his cross daily and follow me. For whoever wants to save his life will lose it, but whoever loses his life for me will save it.*

(Luke 9:23–24)

In other words, following Jesus is not about living to please ourselves but about living lives that will please Him. This is not something that we can do without the help of the Holy Spirit because this kind of life cannot be accomplished through our self-effort. For us to be able to live such a life involves the progressive surrendering of our lives to the Holy Spirit and partnering with Him in the work of transformation that He wants to do in us. He will enable us to become more and more like the One whom we are longing to please. As we do this, we will find ourselves increasingly living the fulfilling, rich and fruitful life[5] that the Bible speaks about. This is God's desire for us.

There is of course a cost involved in following Jesus, and one of the things He said about this was:

> *If anyone comes to me and does not hate his father and mother, his wife and children, his brothers and sisters – yes, even his own life – he cannot be my disciple.*
>
> (Luke 14:26)

I remember that when I first read this verse as a young Christian, I could not relate to it at all because it seemed to be contradicting other passages of Scripture that spoke about loving others in the same way that Jesus loves us. It was a couple of years down the road before I finally understood what Jesus meant. We are to put Jesus first – to love Him more than we loved anyone else.

The willingness of Jesus to lay down His life is demonstrated most clearly in His attitude to the cross,[6] but a careful reading of the Gospels soon makes clear that this attitude permeated His way of life, as well as His teaching, in a variety of ways. One such situation is given in John 13:3–5:

*Jesus knew that the Father had put all things under his power, and that he had come from God and was returning to God; so he got up from the meal, took off his outer clothing, and wrapped a towel round his waist. After that, he poured water into a basin and began to wash his disciples' feet, drying them with the towel that was wrapped round him.*

What an amazing picture we are given here of Jesus' humility! In doing what He did, Jesus demonstrated His servant heart and showed us that someone who has a shepherd's heart will behave in ways that do not fit cultural norms. For example, nowhere does He try to suggest that He was in any way superior to those under His care, as can sometimes be the case with those in authority over us in the various spheres of life. This is reflected in the way that Jesus spoke about and dealt with the different kinds of people that came across His path. Jesus spoke with candour about the religious leaders of His day who thought they were righteous, whilst His own attitude was one of grace and compassion towards those who knew they were not.

In Matthew 23:2–4 we are told that when Jesus was speaking about the religious leaders of His day, He said to those listening to Him:

*The teachers of the law and the Pharisees sit in Moses' seat. So you must obey them and do everything they tell you. But do not do what they do, for they do not practise what they preach. They tie up heavy loads and put them on men's shoulders, but they themselves are not willing to lift a finger to move them.*

Basically, what Jesus did was to tell those listening that since these leaders were in authority over them, they should submit to them. However, He also said that they were not good examples to those under their care as they were putting people in bondage rather than enabling them to find the abundant life[7] that God wanted them to have.

Not only that; as is evident from what Jesus said next, the primary focus of the ministry of these leaders was themselves – their image and reputation – rather than seeking to please God:

*Everything they do is done for men to see: They make their phylacteries wide and the tassels on their garments long; they love the place of honour at banquets and the most important seats in the synagogues; they love to be greeted in the market-places and to have men call them 'Rabbi'.*

(Matthew 23:5–7)

A simple comparison between what Jesus said about the religious leaders and the attitude that He showed towards the Samaritan woman at the well[8] shows us clearly the difference mentioned earlier. However, before we look at the encounter between Jesus and this woman, we need to correct a common assumption that has often been made about her, namely that she was a prostitute. This false belief creates a wrong understanding of her as a person, which then colours our perspective on what happened between her and Jesus. Jesus said that the woman had had five husbands, but what this speaks of most probably is the law of 'levirate marriage'. Basically, when a man died, if his widow had had no children then his brother, or closest male relative (as was the case for Ruth), was required to marry her and produce children for him.[9] The woman at the well was obviously infertile and this was the reason she had been married five times. The man she was currently living with probably did not want to marry her because of it. Since she had not been able to have children she would have been viewed by her community as being cursed by God. This explains why she would have gone to the well at a time of day when she was not likely to encounter many other people from her area.

In speaking to her at all, Jesus broke with convention, but He did so because He was moved by compassion for her. To put it another way, Jesus recognised that she not only was aware of her spiritual condition but also saw her own need for salvation, and this caused Him to reach out to her. In what undoubtedly was a life-changing encounter for this woman, Jesus indicated that He knew what her life had been like and where she was at, and this caused her to open her heart to Him.

From this situation we can see that neither the history nor the circumstances of an individual are issues for Jesus since He can see the heart of that person and is therefore able to identify what their true need is. Having recognised what the woman at the well needed, Jesus then worked with her in such a way that her need was met. Recognising that people are individuals and treating them as such is an important key not just for pastors but for us all. To do otherwise could be damaging to those we are ministering to. In other words, there is no one-size-fits-all approach to life or ministry.

Another important key that we can learn from Jesus is to do with balancing our lives, because otherwise we will either end up with our lives falling apart or burn ourselves out. It is all too easy for pastors, for example, to end up working ridiculously long hours, which not only means that they neglect their families but also that they fail to look after themselves properly. This of course can lead to a multitude of problems for them personally, as well as those they love.

From the life of Jesus, we see that He took time out to pray and to rest. This shows us that there are things we need to do for our personal well-being. We need to prayerfully look at such things as our work/life balance, as well as looking at what the priorities for our life are. Not only that; this is something we need to do again whenever our circumstances change, or we feel led in that direction. Doing so will allow for growth and enable us to press deeper into God.

However, one of the biggest keys of all in terms of navigating our journey into God's heart for us lies in understanding that:

- Jesus lived His life in partnership with the Holy Spirit[10] and we need to learn how to do likewise;
- Jesus only did what He saw the Father doing,[11] and that should be our goal too.

Moreover, just as God had a purpose for Jesus' life and for Esther's, so He has a plan for each one of us, as can be seen from Jeremiah 29:11. Furthermore, we are told in Ephesians 2:10 that:

> *we are God's workmanship, created in Christ Jesus to do good works, which God prepared in advance for us to do.*

The call that God has upon our lives as individuals is linked to, and flows out of, the 'Great Commission'.[12] In other words, we all have a part to play in terms of that Commission, but what that part is will depend on the gifts, abilities and talents that God has put within us. In all of this, it is vital to remember that generally we will not be able to fulfil the call of God on our lives in isolation from the community of God's people. This is clearly taught not just in the Commission itself, but also through the various pictures that God has given us in the Bible depicting His vision for the Church.

Probably one of the clearest of these pictures is the depiction of us corporately as the Body of Christ. Two of the key passages that are vital for understanding the implications of this are Romans 12:4–8 and 1 Corinthians 12:12–31. From these passages we learn, for example, that:

- since we all have different roles, we need each other in order to become a fully functional Body;
- each one of us has different gifts which God has given to us so that we can use them as required to build up the Body;
- when any of us is suffering, it affects us all because we belong to each other.

Moreover, in Ephesians 4:11–13 we read about the 'fivefold ministry':

*It was he who gave some to be apostles, some to be prophets, some to be evangelists, and some to be pastors and teachers, to prepare God's people for works of service, so that the body of Christ may be built up until we all reach unity in the faith and in the knowledge of the Son of God and become mature, attaining to the full measure of the fulness of Christ.*

From these passages we can see something of God's vision for the Church and His plan for us to be equipped to fulfil His call upon our lives. Just as the fivefold ministry is there to equip us, so too was Mordecai with regard to Esther. Not only did he raise Esther, but he also went on mentoring and counselling her even after she became queen. In a sense Mordecai was Esther's shepherd, and as such, we can see him as being a picture of Christ. Moreover, Esther can be seen not just as a picture for us as individual believers of what it means to live for Christ, but also as an image of the corporate Christian life, because she has much to teach us about being a community. From Esther we learn about the importance of commitment, humility, obedience, holiness and fasting, and also about the necessity of taking a stand against evil, rather than passively waiting for someone else to do it. Obviously, we will need to pick our battles prayerfully and our fight will always have, at its core, prayer, as well as perhaps some fasting.

Since 'our struggle is not against flesh and blood',[13] we also need to recognise that:

> *The weapons we fight with are not the weapons of the world. On the contrary, they have divine power to demolish strongholds. We demolish arguments and every pretension that sets itself up against the knowledge of God, and we take captive every thought to make it obedient to Christ.* (2 Corinthians 10:4–5)

Justice will be at the core of any situation where God calls us to take a stand and it will be about prayerfully using our corporate governmental authority to bring His Kingdom into the situation. For example, some of us may find that God leads us to serve Him locally, perhaps fighting the unfair dismissal of an employee of a small business, whilst others may find themselves involved in international affairs, such as brokering a peace deal between two warring nations. It may even be that some find ourselves mediating in disagreements between believers within the life of the church that we belong to and beyond. After all, God's heart is that we should model the love of Christ to those around us and we cannot do that with integrity when there is unresolved conflict in our midst.

However, wherever we go and whatever the Spirit leads us into, we will be there to be the 'salt' and 'light' that Jesus spoke of.[14] To understand what this means let us look first at what salt does, then at the effect of light.

Salt is an antiseptic and as such can be used to cleanse wounds; it melts ice, turning it into water; it preserves and brings out the flavour of food. For us as Christians it speaks of us living in the light of the truth of God's Word in such a way that people's hearts are touched and changed.

Light dispels darkness; it illuminates, guides and warns. This speaks of us standing up for the truth of God's Word in such a way that it enables people to recognise what is wrong in their own lives and in the society in which we live. How we live and what we say should speak of the reality of the God we serve; then people can see the reasons for us living our lives in the way that we do.

Living like this may have hidden and even unexpected costs at times. However, the satisfaction and joy when you see the difference that you are then able to make in people's lives more than makes up for such things. For example, when I lived in East London I had the pleasure of speaking on behalf of a neighbour who had been accused of a crime that they did not commit and seeing them walk free from court afterwards.

What seems to be all too easy for us to forget is that being a disciple of Jesus is about living to please Him, rather than ourselves. In fact, that is what I was referring to when I called this book 'The Esther Strategy'. From my perspective our greatest desire should be to hear Jesus say to us when we go to be with Him, 'Well done, good and faithful servant!'[15] – the same words that the master said to two of the three servants in Jesus' parable of the talents. At times we may need to remind each other that our journey into God's heart for us is preparing us for the wedding of the Lamb described in Revelation 19:6–8:

*Then I heard what sounded like a great multitude, like the roar of rushing waters and like loud peals of thunder, shouting: 'Hallelujah! For our Lord God Almighty reigns. Let us rejoice and be glad and give him glory! For the wedding of the Lamb has come, and his bride has made herself ready. Fine linen, bright and clean, was given her to wear.' (Fine linen stands for the righteous acts of the saints.)*

What a glorious time of celebration that is going to be! Thinking about it should cause us to be eager for the return of our King. It should also spur us on to do as much as possible to see the Kingdom of God advanced in the hope that this will shorten the time before the coming of that glorious day. In the meantime, let us remember the words of Hebrews 10:24 and:

*...let us consider how we may spur one another onto towards love and good deeds.'*

# Endnote References

| 1 | 1 Corinthians 1:26–29 |
| 2 | John 10:1–5, 12–15 |
| 3 | 1 Peter 5:1–3 |
| 4 | Matthew 20:20–28 |
| 5 | John 10:10 |
| 6 | John 10:17–18 |
| 7 | John 10:10 |
| 8 | John 4:7–26 |
| 9 | Deuteronomy 25:5–6 |
| 10 | Luke 4:14–21 |
| 11 | John 5:19 |
| 12 | Matthew 28:16–18 |
| 13 | Ephesians 6:12 |
| 14 | Matthew 5:13–16 |
| 15 | Matthew 25:23a |

# RECOMMENDED BOOKS

David Cross, God's Covering
*(Sovereign World, 2008)*

John Bevere, The Fear of the Lord
*(Creation House, 1997)*

John Bevere, Under Cover
*(Thomas Nelson, 2001)*

Ceil and Moishe Rosen, Christ in the Passover
*(Moody Press, 1978)*

Francis Frangipane, The Three Battlegrounds
*(New Wine Press, 1994)*

Joff Day, Forgive, Release and Be Free
*(Sovereign World, 2004)*

Dan Sneed, The Power of a New Identity
*(Sovereign World, 2000)*

Joy Dawson, Intimate Friendship with God
*(Chosen, 1986)*

Should you want to contact me, my email address is:
JETthepilgrim@gmail.com

# ALSO BY JAN TAYLOR

## A Community of Love
*Jan Taylor*

**This book describes something of what the Bible tells us about the Church being God's family and how He sees it.**

It covers topics such as the Priesthood of all believers, the Body of Christ, the door of worship, the house of prayer, washing one another's feet, the bond of peace, the structure of leadership, shepherding the flock, the value of vision and the importance of discipleship. It has been written for both those who have been Christians for a long time, as well as those who have recently found faith as it is designed to underpin whatever understanding those reading it have of the Church.

ISBN 978-1-911211-91-4

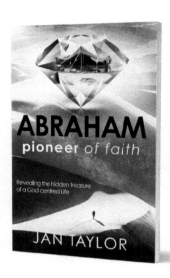

# Abraham: Pioneer of Faith
*Jan Taylor*

**This book is for Christian pilgrims that yearn to discover the treasures to be found deep within our relationship with God.**

Delve into the spiritual principles behind the extraordinary journey of Abraham and see how they can be applied to our life today. As we seek to connect with God, Abraham's story is unpacked to help us progress our own journey of faith into God's heart – just as Abraham journeyed into God's heart for Him.

The author unpacks Abraham's faith issues and examines the call of God on his faith; his real failures and testing; God's covenant with him; his intercession before the Almighty. Vitally, you will see unfold in these pages the fulfilment of God's promises, which to him are looked upon as faith – it is when looking at Abraham's journey that we can truly understand what faith is and the hidden treasure of a God centred life becomes visible.

ISBN 978-1-911211-92-1

Lightning Source UK Ltd.
Milton Keynes UK
UKHW022025270721
387802UK00007B/434